SPRING IN OCTOBER

SPRING IN OCTOBER

THE STORY OF
THE POLISH REVOLUTION 1956

Konrad Syrop

FREDERICK A. PRAEGER
Publishers
NEW YORK

First published in the United States of America
by Frederick A. Praeger, Inc., Publishers,
15 West 47th Street, New York 36, N.Y.

All rights reserved

© by Konrad Syrop 1957

Library of Congress Catalog Card Number 57-14803

For Helen, Mary, Barbara
and Alan

CONTENTS

LIST OF ILLUSTRATIONS

The illustrations numbers 2*a*, *b* and *c*, 8, 5*a* and *b*, 6*a* and *b* are reproduced by courtesy of the Keystone Press; numbers 7*a* and *b* by courtesy of the Polish magazine *Szpilki*; and number 2*d* by courtesy of the Associated Press.

ix

INTRODUCTION

THIS book tells the story of the Polish revolution of 1956, which was overshadowed by the tragic failure of the simultaneous uprising in Hungary. It is a story, but not a history, for it is too soon to see the recent events in full perspective. Some of the pieces of the jigsaw are still missing (and perhaps will never be found), but enough is known already to weave the dramatic events into a coherent narrative and to set them against the relevant background.

The first chapter is in the nature of a historical introduction. Those readers who are fully familiar with Polish history between the years 1939 and 1953 may prefer to begin with the second chapter: this describes the first links in the chain of events that culminated in the dramatic days of October 1956. The story ends with an account of the General Election in January 1957; it has been impossible to include any material that came to light after the end of March 1957.

The reader will find a good many quotations from Polish newspaper articles, poems and speeches, most of them not available elsewhere in English translation, and also a very full account of the proceedings of the VIII Plenum of the Central Committee of the PZPR, a remarkable document, which has not been published outside Poland.

Whenever possible the sources have been indicated, but this book is based not only on published material but also on many conversations with people who have been to Poland recently and with Polish visitors to Britain who must remain anonymous. I have also used my own knowledge of the country and the people and my acquaintance with some of the more important *dramatis personae*.

I have tried throughout to make a clear distinction between

facts and speculation and to avoid any temptation to drama-
tize still further the already dramatic story. My aim has been
to allow events and facts to speak for themselves, but un-
avoidably in assessing them I have had to express some views,
which are entirely my own.

My sincere thanks are due to the many friends and colleagues who have given me help and advice (which I have
not always taken), and especially to Gregory Macdonald and
Stanislaw Faecher for their counsel and assistance.

London, June 1957   K.S.

PART 1

PRELUDE

1

THE LEGACY OF HATE

UNTIL 1954 Poland appeared to be a typical Soviet satellite. The country was run by Moscow trained Communists and was organized on the Soviet pattern; its foreign policy was indistinguishable from that of the Kremlin, and its armed forces were firmly under Russian control. As in the other satellites, the regime was undoubtedly unpopular and the masses dissatisfied with their lot, but outwardly there was little to suggest that Poland was heading for an upheaval.

Political situations, however, are apt to be misleading unless viewed in relation to the past and Poland's past includes not only centuries of fighting against Russia but also deep wounds inflicted by the Soviet Union during the last two decades. These wounds have never ceased to fester and they had an important influence on the developments of 1956.

The memories of more than one hundred years of Russian occupation and of national uprisings ruthlessly put down were still alive in Warsaw, when the Molotov-Ribbentrop pact of 1939 gave Hitler the green light for the invasion of Poland. After seventeen days of the unequal Polish-German war in September 1939, the Russians attacked from the east and occupied half of the country. 'Nothing is left of that monstrous offspring of the Versailles Treaty,' was Molotov's epitaph for Poland.[1]

The Soviet occupation lasted barely two years, but during that time hundreds of thousands of Poles tasted Russian deportation, forced labour camps and prisons; nearly fifteen

[1] In a speech in the Supreme Soviet, October 31, 1939.

3

thousand Polish officers and NCOs, who had been taken prisoner by the Russians during the 1939 campaign, disappeared without trace in the Soviet Union.

In 1941, when the Soviet Union in turn was invaded by Germany, Stalin was forced into a grudging alliance with General Sikorski's Polish Government-in-exile. This Government, from its seat in London, directed the Polish armed forces assembled abroad and the well organized underground movement in Poland. Never wholehearted, because of mutual distrust or effective because of Stalin's obstructive tactics, the Polish-Soviet alliance did not last long. When in April 1943 the Germans announced the discovery of mass graves of thousands of Polish officers in the forest of Katyn, near Smolensk, the Polish Government in London asked for an investigation by the International Red Cross. Stalin replied by breaking off diplomatic relations with the Poles.

The horrible crime at Katyn became a symbol of Polish-Soviet relations. In vain the Russians tried to shift the blame for it on the Germans; they failed to produce any convincing evidence to support this charge and the International War Crimes Tribunal at Nuremberg made no reference to Katyn in its findings. There can be little doubt that the Katyn massacre was the work of the Russians, though it is not certain if the mass execution was a deliberate act of policy or the result of a misunderstood order. In any case the responsibility lay in the cruel and ruthless Soviet system, and the mass graves at Katyn containing the bodies of more than four thousand Polish officers strengthened the already existing wall of hatred between Poles and Russians.

In the midst of the Katyn crisis Sikorski was killed in an air crash and the leader of the Peasant Party, Stanisław Mikolajczyk, took over the Premiership. He made repeated attempts to heal the breach with the Russians, but achieved nothing. Stalin was determined to deal only with a subservient Polish administration. Towards the end of 1943 a

Communist dominated 'Polish Committee of National Liberation' was set up in Russia and the following year, as the German retreat progressed, it established itself in the Polish town of Lublin, which became the temporary capital of Soviet occupied Poland.

In the summer of 1944 the Red Army was approaching Warsaw. Soviet radio stations were broadcasting appeals to the population of the city to rise in arms. The following Soviet broadcast in Polish was monitored in London on the evening of July 29:

> No doubt Warsaw already hears the guns of the battle, which is soon going to bring her liberation. Those who have never bowed their heads to the Hitlerite power will again, as in 1939, join battle with the Germans, this time for decisive action. . . . Poles, the time of liberation is at hand. Poles, to arms! There is not a moment to lose.

The only large and organized Polish force, capable of undertaking effective action against the Germans in Warsaw, was the Underground Army, which remained loyal to the Government-in-exile. Its C.-in-C., Bor-Komorowski, had instructions from London to co-operate with the advancing Russians and though the treatment his army had received from the Soviet authorities in the eastern part of Poland augured badly for the future, he decided to strike in the capital. On August 1 some 40,000 members of the Underground Army seized key points in the city and the Warsaw rising began.

Mikolajczyk was in Moscow at the time, negotiating about the formation of a new Polish Government. He saw Stalin on August 3 and asked for immediate help for Warsaw, especially tanks, artillery and ammunition.[1] Stalin's first reaction was to deny that fighting was taking place in the Polish capital, but he promised to look into the matter. A

---

[1] For a full account see Stanislaw Mikolajczyk, *The Pattern of Soviet Domination* (Sampson Low, London, 1948), pp. 79–82.

few days later Mikolajczyk saw Stalin again and obtained a promise of help, which however was not kept. The Red Army slowed down its advance on the Warsaw front, and when at last it reached the suburbs of the capital on the right bank of the Vistula it made no attempt to cross the river. From a few hundred yards away the Russians watched the desperate battle between the Poles and the Germans.

The only way the Western Allies could send help to Warsaw was by air, but if effective supplies were to be dropped, Allied planes, because of the distance involved, had to refuel on Soviet held airfields; this Stalin refused to allow in spite of repeated appeals from Churchill and Roosevelt.[1] On August 22, 1944, he wrote to the British Prime Minister and the President of the United States: 'Sooner or later the truth about the group of criminals who have embarked on the Warsaw adventure in order to seize power will become known to everybody.'

A revealing sentence. It showed clearly that Stalin was determined not to allow the Poles to 'seize power' in their own country. Warsaw was sacrificed. Without effective outside help the city fought on for sixty-three days and nights, but in the end, when it was quite clear that the Russians would not and the Western Allies could not give effective help, when there was no food left, no ammunition and no medical supplies, Bor-Komorowski surrendered to the Germans. Warsaw was in ruins and a quarter of a million men, women and children had been killed or wounded.

Without firing a shot, Stalin was the victor in the battle of Warsaw. The Polish Underground Army, which stood for its country's independence, had been dealt a mortal blow and within a year Poland was a Soviet satellite. From the Russian point of view this may still turn out to have been a short-sighted victory; while gaining a satellite the Soviet

[1] Winston S. Churchill, *The Second World War*, Vol. VI (Cassells, London, 1954), p. 120.

Union lost a chance of winning a true ally. The Poles could not and did not forget or forgive the Russian behaviour during the battle of Warsaw. Nor did they forget the name of the Soviet C.-in-C. outside the capital—Marshal (then General) Konstantin Rokossovsky.

The last months of the war were taken up by negotiations about the future Government of Poland. The Russians, having converted the Lublin Committee of 'National Liberation' into a Provisional Government, were seeking its recognition by the Western Powers, who were bound by an alliance to the Polish Government in London. At Yalta Stalin managed to persuade Churchill and Roosevelt to accept an arrangement, which looked like a compromise, but in fact amounted to a surrender of Poland to the Soviet Union. The Lublin Government was to be 'broadened' by the inclusion of personalities from Poland and from abroad and was pledged to hold 'free and unfettered elections'. After protracted negotiations Mikolajczyk, who had meanwhile resigned from the Premiership in London, joined the new Government as Vice-Premier and Minister of Agriculture. Three other non-Communists were also given ministerial posts, but Stalin's nominees remained in control; they held 80 per cent of portfolios, including the all important Ministry of Public Security.

Having thus made sure of a subservient Polish Government, Stalin proceeded to redraw the western frontiers of the new satellite. At Teheran he had already obtained Churchill's and Roosevelt's agreement to the incorporation into the Soviet Union of nearly half of pre-war Poland, the lands which lie east of the so-called Curzon line and which the Russians had occupied in 1939 on the basis of the Molotov-Ribbentrop pact. Poland was to be compensated for this loss with a large slice of Germany, but no decision had been taken about the exact extent of Poland's westward extension.

With the exception of the Communists and their followers,

all Polish leaders were vigorously opposed to the loss of eastern Poland, which included the historic cities of Lvov and Vilno, but the decision having been taken by the Big Three, the Poles had little say in the matter. About the compensation at the expense of Germany, Polish leaders were less adamant; most of them welcomed the idea of recovering the lands, which centuries ago had belonged to Poland, but the more responsible among them were against pushing Poland's frontiers too far to the west.[1] Stalin, however, drew the new frontier with Germany along the rivers Oder and Western Neisse; in this way he made certain that in future a genuine Polish-German friendship would be impossible, and that the threat of future territorial demands by Germany would force the Poles always to rely on Soviet support.

Poland has thus paid dearly for the one gift she has received from the hands of Stalin; in terms of foreign policy the price was permanent dependence on the Soviet Union; in human terms it was the uprooting of millions of Poles from the part incorporated in the Soviet Union, moving them further west, and displacing from their homes an even greater number of Germans.

The end of the war saw Poland within her new frontiers, with a Government sponsored by the Russians and dominated by Communists. By definition this could not be a popular administration.

The Polish Communist Party, with its unhappy and unglamorous past, could not hope to rally much popular support. In pre-war years the Party had been declared illegal, which might have attracted to it some of the more adventurous and restless spirits. The temptation to taste the forbidden fruit of Communism was, however, not strong enough to overcome the deep suspicion felt by the overwhelming majority of the people towards this alien ideology and to-

[1] For a full account see Elizabeth Wiskermann, *Germany's Eastern Neighbours* (Oxford University Press for RIIA, London, 1956).

wards the subversive Party, clearly directed by Moscow. The bulk of the politically conscious industrial workers belonged to the democratic Polish Socialist Party, which combined a tradition of patriotism with a vigorous defence of the interests of the working class.

Devoid of popular support, the small underground Communist organization was riddled with police agents and informers. Most of its leaders preferred to live in the apparent safety of the Soviet Union but Stalin, who never trusted Polish Communists, had them executed during his great purges and in 1938 he ordered the Comintern to dissolve the Communist Party of Poland, under the pretext that enemy agents had penetrated into its very leadership. In consequence during the next four years there was not even a vestige of a Communist Party in Poland.

After the German invasion of Russia the Kremlin decided that it could once more make some use of the small band of Polish Communists. In 1942 the Party was revived under the camouflage name of the Polish Workers' Party, hoping thus to attract more popular support. At the beginning it was led by Soviet agents, dropped by parachute behind the German lines, but later the native element, under Wladyslaw Gomulka, began to assert itself. Gomulka was, however, quickly surrounded by Moscow trained Communists, and under their leadership the Party was given the task of governing the new satellite State.

Considering the legacy of hatred of Russia and the dislike of Communism, there were good reasons for the new rulers of Poland to move with circumspection. This they did only for a short while. In January 1947 the first general election, which according to the Yalta agreement was to have been 'free and unfettered', produced by a combination of terror and fraud an overwhelming majority for the Communists and their allies. Mikolajczyk's Polish Peasant Party, which in a really free election would have polled the largest number of votes, was reduced to twenty-eight seats in the *Sejm* (Parliament) composed of 444 deputies.

The way was now clear for a complete Sovietization of Poland. All opponents of Communism were eliminated, forced to flee abroad like Mikolajczyk or browbeaten into compliance. The Socialist Party was merged with the Communists, forming the 'Polish United Workers' Party' (PZPR); other political organizations were either dissolved or allowed to lead an insignificant existence, independent in name only, and forced to follow the Communist line obediently. While formally Poland did not become a single party State the same result was obtained by creating the 'Front of National Unity' controlled by Communists, which included what was left of the old Peasant and Democratic Parties. The Government could thus boast of the existence of three political parties, without running any risk of having to face an organized opposition.

The unavoidable unpopularity of the Government was much increased by psychological blunders committed by those in power. In the country where Stalin's name was anathema they extolled the Soviet dictator as a benefactor of humanity and Poland's friend, teacher and founder of her independence. The hated Soviet system was held up as a shining and unsurpassed example of all virtues.

To give just one typical example of this kind of propaganda, here are some passages from *The Workers' Calendar for 1950*:

The Soviet Union is the hope of mankind. It is the personification of everything that is wise and noble in human culture. The Soviet Union is a benevolent promoter of lofty ideas and is, therefore, loved and admired everywhere.

Comrade Stalin is undoubtedly the greatest social worker of our times and the greatest organizer of the modern world. The Soviet people, and all European peoples, are indebted to Comrade Stalin for his victory over the Hitlerite hordes and the liberation from enslavement. . . .

Perhaps the crowning act was the appointment of the Soviet Marshal Rokossovsky to the post of Poland's Minister of Defence. Though Rokossovsky was of Polish birth and on his appointment reverted to the Polish spelling of his name, he had been brought up as a Soviet citizen and it was he who had commanded the Russian army outside Warsaw during the rising of 1944. It may have been a good military appointment, but it was a psychological blunder.

The Communists were ignoring the fact that Poland had a thousand years' old ties with the West, that spiritually and culturally she was in fact a part of the West, and proud of it. In spite of physical distance, Warsaw and Cracow have always been much closer to Paris, Rome and London than to Moscow. Latin was not only the language of the Church and medieval learning, but for a long time also the language of the educated classes. Later, French became the second language, and in more recent times English gained great popularity. Russian and also German, on the other hand, always brought back the hateful memories of foreign occupation.

For a number of reasons, partly religious, partly political and cultural, panslavist tendencies, which had been in evidence in Bulgaria, Czechoslovakia and Yugoslavia, have never spread to Poland. The ground was particularly ill suited for any attempt to incorporate the Poles in Moscow's orbit. Now this attempt was being made with all possible clumsiness and brutality, as if the Communists were anxious to do everything in their power to increase their unpopularity.

More than 90 per cent of the Poles are Roman Catholic, and the great majority of them are fervently religious. The Communists declared war on religion and the Church. The teaching of religion in schools was abolished, Catholic newspapers were closed, the clergy persecuted and several bishops imprisoned. In 1953 the Primate, Cardinal Wyszynski, was arrested and prevented from exercising the functions of his office.

In a largely agricultural country, where the peasants are passionately attached to their plots of land, the Communists introduced a policy of collectivization. In theory collectivization was voluntary and the Government only provided help and encouragement, but in practice the independent peasant was subjected to strong economic and political pressure to join the collective and if he refused he suffered from penal taxation and police terror.

The Poles are proud of their excellent resistance record under German occupation and of the gallantry of the Polish forces, which had fought at the side of the Allies. The Communists accused leading members of the resistance movement of spying, treason and other crimes and persecuted even the rank and file; soldiers returning from abroad were viewed with suspicion as likely foreign agents and many of them suffered arrest and imprisonment.

Step by step, as the Stalinist system was introduced in Poland, as each class of the population suffered from the terror, privations and humiliations which it brought in its wake, so the hatred of Russia and of the men who, on her behalf, were ruling in Warsaw, reached terrifying intensity. Only the fear of the omnipotent secret police, and the always present shadow of the Red Army prevented a violent explosion.

At the time of Stalin's death the terror was at its highest, the subservience to Moscow at its most complete. It is probably impossible for anyone who did not experience the conditions prevailing in Poland at that time to know what it was really like. Life had the quality of a nightmare reminiscent of George Orwell's *1984*. There was a frightening uniformity, on the surface at least. The dull newspapers were pouring out party propaganda and slogans, which the population also saw on the walls of their factories and offices, which were drummed into their ears by the radio and at the interminable meetings and compulsory 'discussion' groups.

In literature and the arts 'socialist realism' was compulsory. Every book, every poem, every painting was judged by one criterion only: did it serve the interests of the Party. Free speech, or for that matter any form of free expression, was out of the question in public, and could be dangerous in private. Draconic treason laws made the dissemination of simple information impossible, for practically anything could be regarded as a State secret, and the courts which applied the laws were officially described as the instrument of the dictatorship of the proletariat.

Should the public administration of 'socialist justice' be inconvenient, there were also the secret courts which could condemn people without any embarrassing publicity. Thousands were kept in prison by the secret police for years on end, without knowing the charges against them, without being able to inform their families or enlist legal help. Some were tortured to death. In the words of Leon Wudzki, a member of the Central Committee of PZPR, addressing the VIII Plenum on October 20, 1956, there were cases of:

... people who were caught in the streets and released after seven days of interrogation, unfit to live. These people had to be taken to lunatic asylums. Others sought refuge in the asylum to avoid the security police. Men in panic, even honest men, were fleeing abroad to escape our system ... The whole city knew that people were being murdered, the whole city knew that there were cells in which people were kept for three weeks standing in excrements ... cold water was poured on people who were left in the cold to freeze....

In whose hands was this inhuman machine of terror? The answer is somewhat complicated, for the Government of Poland was a curious mixture of direct and indirect rule by the Kremlin. The constitution of the country or the formal organization of the Government gave few clues as to where

13

the real power lay. Until the Kremlin proclaimed the principle of collective leadership, and Poland followed, the situation was in fact tidier, for Boleslaw Bierut combined the functions of Prime Minister and First Secretary of PZPR; on paper and in fact he was the most powerful man in the country. In March 1954, in accordance with the principle of collective leadership, he relinquished the office of Prime Minister, but remained the First Secretary of the Party, and there can be no doubt that he continued to be the satrap of Poland.

The photograph of this stocky, insignificant looking man, with a moustache which gave him a slight resemblance to Hitler, was staring at the people from the walls of all offices, schools and shops, displayed side by side with that of Stalin. He was shown playing with children, talking to workers, addressing meetings; he was described as the founder of People's Poland, her wise guide and philosopher. On the public platform Bierut's performance was not impressive. His speeches lacked fire, they were pedestrian and dull, disclosing little of the cunning and absolute ruthlessness which characterized the man.

Bierut's early life was veiled in mystery and for a good reason. Up to 1944 he was simply a Soviet agent, operating with great secrecy in a variety of countries. He certainly was not one of the leaders of the Polish Communist Party and came into prominence only towards the end of the war.

On January 1, 1944, acting on Soviet instructions, Bierut organized in Warsaw the 'National Council in the Homeland', a Communist dominated mock parliament, which was to provide a semblance of public support for the 'Committee of National Liberation'. It performed this function well, and Bierut went from strength to strength, soon becoming the dominant personality on the Polish scene. The source of his power was in Moscow; he had Stalin's confidence. During his frequent visits to the Kremlin, Bierut received at first hand his political briefing and instructions, first from Stalin and later from Malenkov and Khrushchev.

Among the twelve other members of the Polish Politbureau two occupied positions of special power: under Bierut, Jakub Berman was in charge of the secret police, culture and foreign affairs, while Hilary Minc was the economic chief of the country; both were in the Government. The fourth place in the Polish hierarchy was occupied by Edward Ochab, of whom Stalin had allegedly said that he was 'a good Bolshevik with sharp teeth'. Ochab did not hold a Government post and concentrated on Party affairs; a modest and retiring man, he was little known in the country and few people suspected that he was destined to become Bierut's successor.

The secret police was in the hands of the Minister of Public Security, Stanislaw Radkiewicz, a member of the Politbureau, who took his orders from Bierut and Berman. At his Ministry there were, however, several Soviet 'advisers' and many Russians occupied senior positions in the secret police, so that directives from Beria could and did at times bypass Bierut and the Politbureau.

Over the armed forces the Russians exercised an even more direct control.

The Soviet High Command had direct communications with Marshal Rokossovsky, the Polish Minister of Defence, Deputy Premier and member of the Politbureau. Not only was the Polish army under the command of a Soviet Marshal, but most of the senior posts in the armed services were occupied by Soviet officers, and should this prove inadequate Soviet forces were also stationed in Poland.

Was the monolith without a crack and was the Soviet control absolute? So it seemed. True, in the Politbureau there was one ex-Socialist, Premier Jozef Cyrankiewicz, but he appeared to toe the Party line without reservation. Before the war Cyrankiewicz, one of the coming young men of the Polish Socialist Party, was known for his uncompromising opposition to all forms of totalitarianism. After the German invasion he was active in the Polish underground movement until his arrest in 1941; the remaining years of the war he spent in the infamous concentration camp at Oswiecim (Auschwitz). After his release, to many people's surprise, Cyrankiewicz began to co-operate with the Communists and was one of the architects of the PZPR. Perhaps he did believe Communist statements and was converted by them, or he thought this to be the most promising way of satisfying his personal ambition. Perhaps he saw the best chance of working for Poland from within the Communist dictatorship. Whatever his motives, he did not, and indeed could not disagree with the regime of terror without incurring the penalty. While Stalinism lasted, Cyrankiewicz gave every appearance of being a Stalinist.

The one really significant departure from the Stalinist pattern in Poland was the fate of Wladyslaw Gomulka. This former Secretary General of the Polish Workers' Party had been purged in 1949 for 'nationalist deviation'. He was in prison, but he was alive. Unlike Rajk, Slansky and Kostov he had not been brought to trial, though many of his supporters had to face serious charges and had been sentenced to long imprisonment.

Gomulka was a Communist of many years standing. Born into a working class family in 1905 he joined the Party as a young man and in pre-war Poland served several terms of imprisonment for Communist agitation. His last sentence of seven years' penal servitude, which he received in 1936, kept him in the safety of a Polish prison while Stalin liquidated the Communist Party and its leaders.

At the outbreak of war Gomulka was released and took part in the defence of Warsaw in September 1939. When the country was overrun by the Germans he decided to form an underground Communist organization and together with several friends sent a message to Moscow asking for support.

There was no reply, but Gomulka went ahead on his own. Only after the German invasion of Russia Soviet agents began to arrive by parachute and took over the small Communist organization. Without Gomulka's knowledge they were engaged in spying on the Polish underground movement, which was loyal to the Government-in-exile, and they denounced some of its members to the Gestapo. In the autumn of 1943, when the Soviet agent in charge was killed, and there was apparently a break in wireless communications with Moscow, Gomulka was elected to lead the Polish Workers' Party. On discovering his predecessors' contacts with the Germans he was outraged and put an immediate end to all collaboration with the Gestapo.

More Soviet agents were sent into Poland, including Bierut, but Gomulka was too popular in the Party to be displaced. When, in the wake of advancing Soviet armies, a Communist administration was introduced in Poland, Gomulka remained the First Secretary of the Party and was given the important post of Deputy Premier in charge of the Western Territories. In this latter capacity he was reported to have clashed with Marshal Rokossovsky (who was at the time in command of the Soviet occupation troops in the area) over the question of the dismantling and looting of German property, which Gomulka was anxious to preserve for Poland.

Gomulka, judging by all accounts, was a fanatical Communist with a violent temper. Mikolajczyk, in his book *The Pattern of Soviet Domination*, described how, in the course of a political argument, Gomulka threatened him with a pistol. But Gomulka was also a Polish patriot who believed that Poland should follow her own road to Socialism and was opposed to the blind imitation of the Soviet example. He quickly came into conflict with his Stalinist colleagues, because he argued that there was no need for a single party dictatorship and that the pace of agricultural collectivization

17

and of the industrialization of the country ought to be adjusted to Poland's needs. Writing in the official Party monthly *Nowe Drogi* in April 1947, he declared: 'We have chosen our own Polish road to development, which we have named a People's Democracy. Along this road, and under such conditions, the dictatorship of a single party is neither essential nor has it any purpose. . . . Poland can and is following her own path.'

This was precisely what Poland was not allowed to do. After the expulsion of Yugoslavia from the Cominform, Gomulka was accused of 'Titoism', 'bourgeois nationalism' and other crimes in the Stalinist code. He was immediately deprived of his posts in the Party and the Government, but his arrest did not take place until July 1951. All his more prominent followers shared his fate and languished in prison, but few of them were brought to trial and none were executed.

Except for the treatment of Gomulka and his associates, Poland appeared to be a perfect and completely cowed Soviet satellite. Surrounded by the Soviet Union and territories controlled by Moscow, with Soviet troops stationed inside the country, Poland was sealed off from the west as completely and efficiently as any other part of the Soviet empire. And yet, the iron curtain was not quite impregnable and there remained one direct link with the outside world—the radio. In common with other Communist countries, Poland was vigorously jamming the broadcasts coming from the west. A vast network of special stations was engaged in emitting a noise which was to drown the western transmissions. Costly and efficient as it was, it never succeeded in obliterating the Polish broadcasts of the BBC, the Voice of America and Radio Free Europe.

During the height of the Stalinist nightmare the Poles could and did keep in touch with freedom. They had done so during the terrible years of the German occupation, when the BBC, and later also *Radio Polskie* operating from London and the Voice of America, provided them with a direct link. Now, subjected not only to terror but also to persistent, all pervasive Communist propaganda, they turned to the voices from the west for a psychological antidote, for truth, for a breath of fresh air. They found it and it helped them to survive without surrendering their minds.

2

THE FALL OF THE POLISH BERIA

IN the summer of 1953, after the elimination of Beria, when
the power of the Soviet secret police was broken, a chain
reaction began which was to lead to the gradual elimination
of terror from the political life of Poland and to the October
revolution. However, the Polish Communist leaders were not
anxious to follow the Soviet example of relaxation; they had
good reasons to view with apprehension the likely consequences. Towards the end of 1953 the Russians circulated
to all the satellites a memorandum on the excesses of the
MVD, but it was only some six months later that a Polish
delegation, led by one of the secretaries of the Party, Franciszek Mazur, himself an ex-NKVD man, arrived in Moscow
to learn how the Soviet Union was reorganizing its secret
police. As we can see, the Polish Communists did not regard
the problem as urgent. Their own secret police chief, Stanislaw Radkiewicz, was an obedient tool of Bierut and Berman,
and whatever his connections with Beria might have been, he
was fulfilling a useful function in ruthlessly suppressing all
opposition.

Meanwhile, in December 1953, two high ranking officials
of the Polish Security Police arrived in Berlin on a special
mission; their task was to arrange with their East German
colleagues for the silencing of a Polish Communist who had
escaped to the Federal Republic. Not only did the mission
fail to achieve its objective, but it was destined to accelerate
the process of purging the Polish security police.

One of the two officials from Warsaw crossed into West

Poland showing the pre-war and post-war boundaries

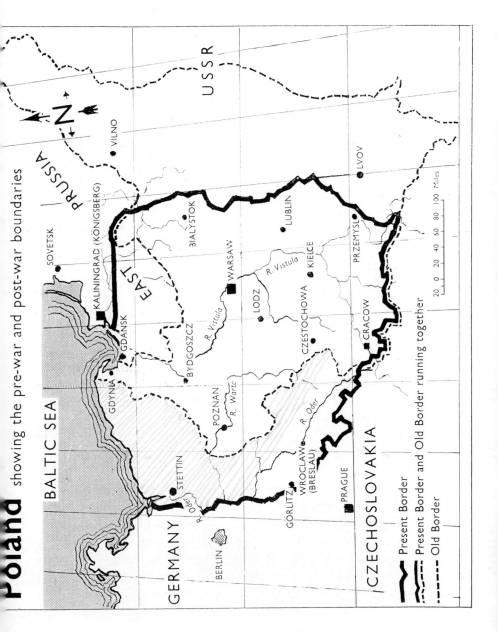

I.

2. *a*. Wladyslaw Gomulka.

2. *b*. Joseph Cyrankiewicz.

2. *c*. Edward Ochab.

2. *d*. Cardinal Wyszynski.

Berlin and asked the Americans for asylum. There must have been surprised faces around him when he revealed his identity—he was Jozef Swiatlo, the Assistant Director of the X Department of the Warsaw Ministry of Public Security and a Lieutenant-Colonel in the Polish Security Police.

Swiatlo was allowed to go to the United States and after several months, during which the Americans were checking his story, he broke his silence, gave a press conference in Washington on September 29, 1954, and began to broadcast to Poland. Radio Free Europe, the American financed broadcasting service, devoted nearly one hundred and fifty short programmes to the Swiatlo revelations,[1] while the Polish Service of the BBC gave a full summary of the more important statements.

What could Swiatlo tell that would justify so much publicity directed back to Poland whence he had escaped? The answer lay in his official position, which gave him access to particularly interesting and important information, for the X Department of Ministry of Public Security, of which he had been Assistant Director, was responsible for keeping an eye on the higher echelons of the Communist Party. Swiatlo himself had been the guardian of the secret personal files of the members of the Politbureau, which were at the disposal of the First Secretary, Boleslaw Bierut. Because of his position of trust he was able to learn a great deal about the inner working of the Party and the control exercised by the Russians. Swiatlo could thus speak with authority on many points, which previously had been the subject of guesswork or deduction.

From Swiatlo we have a confirmation of the Soviet system of control of Poland and of the chain of command.

Under Soviet direction Bierut was the undisputed ruler of

[1] A full summary of the Swiatlo broadcasts was published in *News from Behind the Iron Curtain* (Free Europe Committee Inc, New York, March 1955).

Poland, and next to him came Berman and Minc, but even they were not trusted completely and compromising evidence about them was kept in Swiatlo's files, in case Bierut needed to bring his assistants to heel. The picture of personal relations between the top Communists, painted by Swiatlo in much detail, was particularly nauseating. Even if one ignored the sordid part of their private lives, one was left with the inescapable conclusion that here was a group of utterly ruthless and utterly dishonest men who stopped at nothing in order to fulfil the orders of their Soviet masters and to foster their own private interests.

Only one leading Communist came out unscathed—Wladyslaw Gomulka, who Swiatlo himself had arrested in July 1951. Swiatlo described Gomulka's dignified and courageous behaviour. Gomulka had not only refused to confess the imaginary crimes of which he was being accused, but threatened that, should he be brought to trial, he would tell publicly the full story of Bierut's and his associates' past, how they allowed their friends and comrades in Russia to be eliminated in the pre-war purges, how they collaborated with the Germans during the war, how they plotted against each other. . . . According to Swiatlo the fear of Gomulka's testimony, combined with a complete failure to obtain or manufacture any convincing evidence of his alleged collaboration with the West, accounted for the fact that he was never brought to trial. This does not explain, however, why Gomulka was not executed secretly.

The most important part of the Swiatlo revelations consisted of a complete disclosure of the methods of the security police which operated outside the law. He described in detail how, on the orders of the Russians or Bierut and Berman, innocent people were arrested, how they were tortured or tricked into confessions, how the public or secret trials were rigged in advance.

The Swiatlo broadcasts came at a moment when the first

stirrings were already taking place in Poland as a result of the death of Stalin and the milder wind from Moscow. There can be little doubt that the revelations, particularly regarding the activities of the secret police, came as a shock to members of the Party. All, but the most naive of them, must have had their suspicions before, but these were now amply confirmed by someone who was in a position to know; the truth turned out to be worse than their own worst fears.

The authorities were forced to act. On October 25, 1954, four weeks after the Swiatlo press conference in Washington, an official communiqué was issued in Warsaw:

Following an inspection ordered by the State Authorities in the middle of 1953 certain cases were brought to light of a gross violation of the people's rule of law. . . . The authorities detected Jozef Swiatlo as an agent provocateur of the US secret service. . . . Taking advantage of the absence of proper supervision, he selected certain persons and caused them to be arrested on false charges. One of the persons so arrested was an American citizen, Hermann Field, the case against whom was deliberately framed by Swiatlo with particularly provocative perfidy.

This clumsy attempt to turn the tables was not enough to save the secret police system. The rank and file of the Party were deeply disturbed and the leaders, most of whom could not have much peace of mind, had to do something drastic. Two articles in the official Party daily, *Trybuna Ludu*, published at the end of October, foreshadowed the impending changes. The security police were accused of having set up 'a State within a State', while the Party did not exercise the necessary control. The paper demanded that the abuses should be stopped, the guilty punished and the rule of law fully restored.

Yet, nothing happened for several weeks and the reason, as we now know, was dissension among the Party. In his remarkably frank speech two years later Ochab said:

Let me remind you of the meeting of the Party 'activ' in

November 1954, when the leadership found itself in virtual isolation. The proposals of the leadership, though they were on the right lines, were much too limited in relation to the needs of the situation.[1]

It is probable that the Politbureau itself was divided and that November 1954 marked the beginning of the rift among its thirteen members. This would explain the further delay, for it was only on December 8 that an official communiqué announced the abolition of the Ministry of Public Security. Following the Soviet pattern, its functions were divided between the Ministry of the Interior and a newly set up Committee of Public Security, responsible to the Council of Ministers. Stanislaw Radkiewicz, the Minister of Public Security, who for ten years had been in charge of political terror, was given the Ministry of State Farms. This was not only a political demotion, but in view of the chronic difficulties in agriculture, an appointment which was doomed to end in failure. Radkiewicz retained, however, his seat in the Politbureau.

The December issue of *Nowe Drogi*, the official Party monthly, which went to press a few days later, contained a six-thousand word article about the role of the secret police and foreshadowed further important changes. Declaring that the reorganization was in keeping with the new situation in the country and arose out of the need 'for a further democratization of the State' it stressed that the administration of justice must be left to independent courts. The article also contained a highly significant passage pointing out that political 'deviation' should not be equated with treason.

Few people at the time recognized this last remark as the signal for the release of Wladyslaw Gomulka. This came on Christmas Eve 1954, though it was kept secret until April 1956.

The struggle within the Party gathered momentum. When

[1] Published in *Nowe Drogi* (Warsaw, October 1956), p. 115.

While Gomulka remained in prison

the III Plenum of the Central Committee of the PZPR met in Warsaw, Bierut delivered yet another attack on the security police. In his speech on January 21 he said that 'the control of the Party leadership over the entire field of activity of the Ministry of Public Security and the scope of its tasks had been inadequate' and he spoke of 'the impermissible atmosphere' in some sections of the former Ministry. This statement, coming from the man under whose orders the security police had been acting, did not satisfy the Central Committee. Once more the leadership found itself in isolation, and once more it was forced to go further than it wanted. No sooner was the Plenum over than a purge of the security police began.

On January 27 it was officially announced that the Deputy Minister of Public Security, Roman Romkowski, had been dismissed and expelled from the Party together with two departmental heads of the Ministry, Anatol Fejgin of the X Department (who had been Swiatlo's chief) and Jacek Rozanski of the investigation department. Rozanski was placed under arrest and later sentenced to five years' imprisonment. Many other dismissals and arrests followed in quick succession.

The upheaval was not limited to the security police. In his speech to the III Plenum, Bierut describing the main shortcomings of the Party defined them as 'the lack of collectivity in Party leadership, the violation of the principles of democracy inside the Party, the ignoring of criticism and self-criticism, and the use of bureaucratic methods'.

The press developed Bierut's theme in a remarkably frank manner. The Party daily *Trybuna Ludu*, for instance, declared on February 4: 'the false notion that political wisdom is concentrated in the narrow circle of the higher Party organs' must be eradicated.

The decisions of the III Plenum were never published. They contained a directive for the liberalization of the system, or 'democratization' to use the Communist term which later became very fashionable. It was not without significance that the publication of this programme was withheld, for the majority of the Politbureau were anxious to slow down rather than encourage liberalization, but they were prepared to allow a certain freedom of criticism.

Describing the decisions of the III Plenum in *Nowe Drogi* (February 1955) one of the newly elected secretaries of the Party, Jerzy Morawski, made it clear that that discussion was being encouraged not for its own sake, but in order to strengthen the Party. 'We want,' he wrote, 'people to express their doubts and reservations with greater courage, so that the doubts can be dispelled and the reservations overcome.'

In the March issue of the same journal one of the leading Communist writers, Leon Kruczkowski, appealed for a new and a more propitious atmosphere for the ideological activities of the intellectuals, and he called for 'a great candid discussion, which goes right down to fundamentals and into which we must draw those who have kept silent during the past few years, though we know full well that they have a great deal to say'.

It would be wrong to conclude from these quotations that Polish intellectuals had been silent. In fact, already a few months before these invitations were issued, they had been conducting a vigorous discussion on the subject of 'socialist realism', which at times came perilously near to a discussion on Communism itself. The 'thaw' declared by Moscow, and the warmer winds accompanying it, had not been without effect in Poland. As if waking from a long winter sleep Polish intellectuals were rubbing their eyes, and gently at first, with increasing vigour later, were saying that they did not like what they saw.

'The writer is paralysed when he knows that every word he writes will be scrutinized, and examined carefully, according to one decisive criterion—whether or not he has exposed himself.' These words, by a prominent young writer, Jan Kott, appeared in the leading Warsaw literary weekly *Nowa Kultura* on March 6, 1955.

Soon the discussion was getting out of control and the Party had to make a determined effort to steer it into 'correct' channels. In the June issue of *Nowe Drogi* a long article by Stafan Zolkiewski tried to set a new course for the intellectuals. It admitted many of the past errors with apparent frankness, e.g. 'The greatest mistake of our cultural policy has been the use of the easy and vulgar method of issuing orders instead of the necessary and difficult Party guidance of the ideo-political development.' 'A serious mistake was cutting ourselves off from many parts of the world, from the progressive cultural achievements. . . .'

Having admitted that much, the Party journal attacked writers who hold the view 'that the evil, which we are fighting, is an inherent characteristic of our system', and those who believe that Marxism-Leninism 'is only an intellectual concept, which cannot be sufficient to a "complete man", who also needs metaphysics to appeal to his heart and imagination'. The expression of such views was harmful, decreed *Nowe Drogi*; the discussion should continue, but it should deal with the question as to how cultural life could be guided, while avoiding the mistakes of the past.

When the Association of Writers met in June 1955, it was addressed by its Deputy Chairman, Jerzy Putrament, in these words:

The ideological confusion within our literary community has reached . . . alarming proportions. . . . To bring this chaos to an end two operations must start immediately. First, bourgeois recidivism must be repulsed from our ideas concerning the development of art. Second, any weakness in true understanding of socialist realism must be removed.

The tough line against the critics who went too far was further developed during the summer. The editor of the official Party daily published an article in the Moscow *Pravda* of August 24, 1955, in which he declared that the PZPR 'has opened a resolute struggle against relapses into bourgeois ideology on the cultural front', but made it clear that the battle was by no means over yet.

Indeed, three days before that article appeared in Moscow, a virtual bombshell had exploded on the political and literary front in Poland. *Nowa Kultura* of August 21, 1955, published Adam Wazyk's long *Poem for Adults*.[1] This work by a leading Communist poet was a sweeping condemnation of the regime, a cry of protest against the lying propaganda of the Party. They had said, wrote Wazyk:

> Under Socialism
> a cut finger does not hurt.
> They cut their finger,
> they felt pain.
> They lost faith.

Poem for Adults was full of revulsion against the injustices, the poverty and immorality bred by the system, against broken promises, boredom, inefficiency and lawlessness of Bierut's Poland. It ended with a demand

> for a clear truth
> for the bread of freedom,
> for burning reason,
> for burning reason.

Wazyk added that he was making these demands through the Party, but the Party, not without reason, interpreted the poem as an attack on itself. The editor of *Nowa Kultura* was dismissed, and *Poem for Adults* was violently attacked in the press. Wazyk himself remained at liberty, still a member of the Party but forced into silence. He became a popular hero; copies of the *Poem for Adults* were circulating from hand to hand avidly read by thousands and when Wazyk entered a Warsaw café he was greeted with applause.

[1] A translation of this poem by Lucjan Blit appeared in *The Twentieth Century* (London, December 1955).

The regime got more than it had bargained for. The discussion, once opened, was not easy to close without stern measures, and these the leadership was not prepared to adopt. There were warnings to the intellectuals, instructions to editors and censors, and yet the debate continued. It was less outspoken than the *Poem for Adults*, but in subtle ways it questioned many of the principles on which rested the power of the Party. There were public demands for more freedom for the newspapers, for more independence for thinkers, for less slavish praise of everything Soviet, for less secrecy about the economic conditions in the country.

To people living in Poland it seemed that a strong wind of freedom was beginning to blow across the plains, but these were only the first stirrings of a gentle breeze, compared with the hurricane which was to come the following year.

3

THE EARTHQUAKE

AT the beginning of 1956 there were already heavy clouds
gathering on the Polish horizon. The leadership of the PZPR
was subject to external and internal pressures. Moscow had
decreed a thaw in its relations with the West, and was setting
the tone for a somewhat more liberal policy in internal
matters. Many members of the Central Committee of the
PZPR were demanding far-reaching reforms, which the
Politbureau was unwilling to undertake. But was the Politbureau united? Even in Western countries it is difficult for
an outside observer to know what is happening at private
meetings of the inner councils of a party; in a 'people's democracy' it is quite impossible, and we are reduced to speculation as to what took place within the Polish Politbureau.

It is fairly obvious why the Politbureau found itself
isolated from the rest of the Party; its members were in a
better position than anyone else to realize how unpopular the
system was in Poland, how inefficiently it worked and how
serious was the economic situation. Yet, they themselves had
created the system and were responsible for it. Bierut,
Berman and Minc were the architects of Stalinism in Poland,
they had held supreme power for a number of years, and it
must have been exceedingly difficult for them to introduce
changes, which clearly implied their own failure. In their
attitude they were no doubt supported by the majority of the
Politbureau, but it is reasonable to assume that already at
that stage some of its thirteen members were pressing for reforms. This would explain the vacillating attitude to the

press, the encouragement of criticism on the one hand, and its suppression on the other.

After the tougher line, which followed the publication of Wazyk's *Poem for Adults*, there was a new relaxation of censorship in January 1956. Wazyk's demand for truth was taken up again. On January 15 *Życie Warszawy*, a Communist daily, published an article entitled *The Moral Strength of Truth*. The author was Professor Julian Hochfeld, an ex-Socialist and now a PZPR deputy to the *Sejm* (the Polish Parliament). He wrote:

What hampers the development of Socialism is the persistent inefficacy of most criticism, even when those who are criticized admit the shortcomings. We must recognize that repeated experiences count for more than all the beautiful principles put together. If, in spite of all criticism, a bad organization of labour in factories turns into fiction our socialist principles of rewarding the workers, then one cannot expect the workers to look upon these principles as anything but empty words. . . . Criticism of evil phenomena must be effective, or it will only result in moral numbness. . . .

Professor Hochfeld went on to postulate that 'those who direct our public life, from the highest to the lowest, must be really responsible not only to their superiors, but to the masses and to public opinion'. Here was undisguised heresy, proclaimed publicly in a Communist newspaper. Professor Hochfeld's argument was taken up by the literary weekly *Nowa Kultura*, which published on January 22 an article demanding that the *Sejm*, which had become a mere rubber stamp for Government decrees, should fulfil its constitutional function of controlling the Government and criticizing it; the press should report in full parliamentary debates and questions.

At the same time the weekly paper of students and young writers *Po Prostu* (Plain Speaking) developed a vigorous and refreshing policy of honest criticism. In the issue of January 22, for instance, appeared *Confessions of a converted cynic*, a bitter article by a young journalist, Jerzy Urban, who wrote:

Do you understand? In the name of higher aims . . . the most normal human emotions were being scrupulously suppressed. For the good of socialism I was deprived of my most effective weapon —my sensitivity and the possibility to write about these matters (social evils). I lied doubly—by not writing about things that mattered and by varnishing the truth. And what is worse, I and others believed in the sense and the reason of these lies.

Urban's *Confessions* showed the mental confusion among young Communists, which was soon to become even worse confounded. He wrote: 'What are we to love? What are we to hate? Theoretically we know the answer, but already we can feel neither passionate love, nor passionate hatred.'

The Party and its leaders were still above criticism, and another writer, in *Nowa Kultura* of February 19, put it in these words: 'I feel that we are standing in front of an impassable wall, an impregnable fortress, an unattainable greatness, accountable to "God and History" alone.'

When these words were being printed, the walls of the impregnable fortress were already shaking—the XX Congress of the Soviet Communist Party was taking place in Moscow. It brought in its wake three events, the combined effect of which was that of an earthquake. The three events were: the rehabilitation of the pre-war Polish Communist Party, Khrushchev's 'secret' speech denouncing Stalin and the death of Boleslaw Bierut.

On February 19 *Trybuna Ludu* carried the following announcement:

In 1938 the Executive Committee of the Communist International decided to dissolve the Communist Party of Poland following an accusation that enemy agents had penetrated its leadership.

It has now been found that this accusation was based on evidence fabricated by provocateurs who have since been unmasked.

Having examined all the relevant evidence the Central Committees of the Communist Parties of the Soviet Union, Italy, Bulgaria and Finland, together with the Central Committee of PZPR, have come to the conclusion that the dissolution of the Communist Party of Poland was unjustified. . . .

Commenting on this curious document, the March issue of *Nowe Drogi* stated that the joy at the rehabilitation of the old Communist Party was accompanied by pain and anger and added that 'in the accounting, which is taking place in the conscience of many Communists, it should be remembered that the exposing of falsehood, the destruction of myths, and the breaking of the seals of secrecy has all now begun in a resolute and courageous manner'.

While the implications of this new move were sinking in, *Trybuna Ludu* on March 10 carried the first echo of Khrushchev's speech denouncing Stalin. Three days later, without any warning, it was announced that Bierut, who had been in Moscow attending the XX Congress, had died there after a severe illness. Not unnaturally, many people in Poland concluded that he had been murdered by the Russians. Premier Cyrankiewicz did little to dispel this impression when he described Bierut's death as 'a blow that took us all by surprise'.

The rumours that Bierut had been a victim of the Russians gave him a short period of posthumous popularity in Poland and thousands of people, who hated communism, paid him homage while his body lay in state in Warsaw. During the funeral many speeches were made, some of them of political significance. 'Comrade Bierut is dead, but our Party lives, united and monolithic', was the pious hope of the Chairman of the Council of State, Alexander Zawadzki. 'During his illness he discussed with us on the telephone decisions that were to be taken on his return, in order to improve gradually, and already this year, the condition of those who are least well paid', said Premier Cyrankiewicz. 'Burning with Polish patriotism, always a Communist and a Leninist, Comrade

Bierut was full of courage and strength', said Nikita Khrushchev on behalf of the Soviet Union. Bierut, the arch-Stalinist of Poland, was clearly to be excluded from the accusations now levied against his master: the Bierut myth was to remain intact.

In the presence of Khrushchev the VI Plenum of the Central Committee met in Warsaw on March 20 to appoint Bierut's successor. A laconic official communiqué announced that Edward Ochab had been unanimously elected First Secretary. Though, according to Swiatlo, Ochab had been groomed for the role of Bierut's successor, his appointment, in the circumstances prevailing at the time, was somewhat surprising. Ochab was not an outstanding leader, he did not command popular support either within or outside the Party, and his rise to the Politbureau only two years previously was allegedly due to Stalin's good opinion of him. Khrushchev must have shared Stalin's high regard for Ochab, and thought the fifty-year-old Communist a safe choice for the key post in Poland.

When Ochab's appointment was announced, the 'earthquake' was already shaking the Communist régime, threatening its very foundations. *Trybuna Ludu* of March 10, in a masterly understatement, described the eruption of doubts and questioning as 'a great process of re-educating our Party, a process which is very difficult for every one of us'. Some three weeks later, the same official newspaper was forced to be more explicit. One of its readers had written to ask how could one be sure that the conclusions of the XX Congress were not yet another mistake, and this was quoted in the issue of March 29, together with the following comment:

What should we believe and whom should we believe? What is true and what is false? There is nothing strange in those questions. Today many people think on these lines: if in the past I could believe in lies and accept them as truth, who can guarantee that what I accept as truth today is not just another lie?

34

The only advice the official paper offered was: 'It is not blind faith, but reason and conviction that must decide what is right.'

Po Prostu was more outspoken. Jan Stanislawski, a young Communist, deeply ashamed by the revelations about Stalin, wrote on March 25: 'I have a grievance against the men who, for reasons unknown to me, have led me to my present humiliation, to the men who allowed the "cult of the individual" to establish itself, and who supported it. I ask: what did the comrades at the top do to prevent the "cult of the individual", which they now condemn?' Having asked this embarrassing question, the author went on to state his even more embarrassing conclusion: 'For me there are no more authorities. There are only people. They must be accountable to other people.'

Stanislawski was writing in a fury. His staccato questions and statements followed each other without much order. 'There is chaos in my head,' he confessed, adding that the readers of the paper were no doubt in a state of similar confusion. He ended simply: 'I can see one conclusion emerging from this chaos, and you must see it too: there are no authorities any more, and this applies from the district secretary to the First Secretary of the Central Committee.'

This was no isolated outburst. *Nowa Kultura* (April 15, 1956) printed a letter from an eighteen-year-old student of Warsaw Polytechnic, Michal Bruk, who described in moving words how his faith had been repeatedly shattered. His brother had fought in the Home Army and was killed by the Germans—he was a hero to Michal, but soon the boy was told that the Home Army had been traitors. He turned to religion, but Party propaganda made him lose his faith. In 1953 he became a Communist and refused to believe what his family and friends told him about the secret police terror, about Stalin's dictatorship and about the falsification of history by the Party. Now all these accusations had turned out to be true and Bruk wrote:

I am ashamed of all of you, and above all of myself because of my stupidity and credulity. I know no longer how to raise my head . . . for I have no foundation for believing anything. . . . Perhaps now will begin the genuine realization of Communist ideas . . . but probably I will not be with you, because I have no reason to trust you. . . . I wish you all success, but please do not be surprised at us young people.

The reaction among young Communists was most violent, but the older generation was also suffering from shock. A distinguished Communist poet, Leon Pasternak, wrote in *Nowa Kultura* (April 1, 1956):

> Our brows are marked with the stigma of injustice,
> Our words meet with distrust,
> And feeling deceived, many have left us.
> Perhaps you or I have never been blind,
> But we are guilty,
> My friend.

Unlike the young, Pasternak seemed to be clinging to his Communist faith, in spite of the 'inhuman weight of suffering' and though 'a century will not heal these wounds', he wanted to go 'forward and forward', but it was difficult for the reader to escape the impression that this urge to advance was based on desire to get away from the past.

Wazyk was allowed to write again after the long enforced silence and he published a moving *Message to a Friend* in *Nowa Kultura* on April 8, 1956. He, too, spoke of 'the festering wounds which will take a long time to heal', and expressed the bitterness and disillusionment experienced by Communists.

A veritable orgy of soul-searching and self-criticism swept Poland. The satirical weekly *Szpilki* printed on April 1 a cartoon showing a railway carriage, with the guard removing the notice 'Do NOT lean out' and replacing it by 'Do lean out'; this became the slogan of the day. Economists, politicians, journalists and, most of all, poets and novelists, were ques-

a. Soldiers and strikers fraternize near the Security Police building during the Poznan riots.

b. Scene outside the radio jammer after the first day of the riots. Wrecked amming equipment in the foreground and in the background a tram over-turned to form a barricade.

4. A million pilgrims at the national religious shrine, Czestochowa.

tioning the established dogmas, complaining about lack of freedom and about the low living standards of the workers. All this criticism went much further in Poland than in any other Communist country.

On April 6 Ochab, in his first major public speech since he became First Secretary, made an attempt to regain control of the situation. He readily admitted past mistakes, which he attributed to the 'cult of the individual' and to the nefarious influence of Beria and expressed himself in favour of a more open public life. 'I am convinced,' he said, 'that we can tell the masses, and in particular the Party, much more and much more fully than has been done up to now. It appears that we have been over cautious. There was too much reticence in order that the enemy would not learn about our troubles.'

At the same time Ochab came out strongly against the more outspoken critics. 'Some comrades seem to be losing their sense of proportion and their sense of balance between what is justified criticism and utterances expressing a point of view that cannot be advantageous to the Party. There are people who in public, in the press, and not through the Party, come out against the Party. This shows an unhealthy, anarchistic tendency. . . . They are concerned with the Party in words only; in actual fact they hit out at the Party.'

This 'tendency to hysteria' was, according to Ochab, due to the profound shock caused by the revelations about Stalin, and the remedy was a collective effort for the democratization of public life, which could be achieved only if members exercised self-control and preserved unity. Ochab admitted that the decisions of the III Plenum of January 1955, formulating the 'correct policy of democratization', had been insufficiently implemented because the leadership did not pursue it with sufficient vigour.

Turning to economic matters, Ochab spoke of the failure to increase agricultural production and the real incomes of workers. He promised that efforts in that direction would be redoubled, but warned that the possibilities of achieving an improvement in the current year were modest.

The most sensational part of Ochab's speech concerned Wladyslaw Gomulka, the former Secretary General of the Party. Ochab announced Gomulka's release from prison, without mentioning that this had taken place more than a year previously, and said that the former leader had been cleared of the charges of treason. He added, however, that the Party had not abandoned the struggle against Gomulka's ideological concept.

The same speech revealed the release from prison, complete rehabilitation and readmission to Party membership of twenty-six other persons imprisoned before 1953 on the basis of false charges. Among them were many supporters of Gomulka, including Generals Kirchmayer and Waclaw Komar. The puzzling feature was the difference in the treatment of Gomulka himself and that of his associates; if the latter were readmitted to the Party, why not readmit Gomulka as well? It is possible that the offer had been made to Gomulka, but he turned it down, demanding more than the mere return of his Party card. It is also possible that some of the members of the Politbureau like Berman and Minc, who had been violently opposed to Gomulka, would not agree to his return to the fold.

Ochab's speech did not restore the Party's control over public opinion. Some newspapers allowed themselves even veiled unfriendly references to the Soviet Union, and there were open demands for the rehabilitation of the members of the former underground army. The agitation, which had so far been mainly confined to the upper reaches of the Party, the intelligentsia and the press, was now spreading to all classes. The rank and file of the Party was beginning to exert strong pressure on the leadership. On April 17 *Trybuna Ludu* wrote:

We are reviewing the list (of our mistakes), each of us in his own conscience, and in talks which have never been so long or so passionate. We are rendering this account of our mistakes at hundreds of Party meetings, in which thousands of Communists speak. . . . These matters are close to the whole nation, and the whole nation speaks of them today. Angry and impassioned words are heard, words of bitterness, pain and sharp criticism. The mistakes committed have cost us dearly, and there is a natural and healthy desire to reach the source of evil and eradicate it once and for all.

To placate public opinion, the Party announced a further purge of the secret police and of the administration of justice. On April 20 the civil and military Prosecutors-General were dismissed, and at the same time a far-reaching amnesty bill was published; this provided for the release of some 30,000 prisoners and the suspension of proceedings against another 40,000 accused of ordinary or political crimes. Three days later the arrests were announced of the former Deputy Minister of Public Security, Romkowski, and of the head of the X Department, Fejgin. In quick succession the public learned that the former head of the Investigation Department of that Ministry, Jacek Rozanski, would be retried because the five-year sentence passed on him in December 1955 was too lenient, and that Radkiewicz had been dismissed from the Ministry of State Farms. Also dismissed were the Minister of Justice, and his deputy, and the Ministers of Culture and Higher Education. It was significant that all the purged individuals were most closely associated in the public mind with the worst Stalinist abuses and also that they had all worked under the direction of Berman.

During the spring session of the *Sejm*, which met in Warsaw from April 23 to 28, there was, for the first time, something resembling a genuine parliamentary debate, with many deputies criticizing various aspects of Government activity. For the first time, also, the voting was not unanimous and five deputies opposed a Government bill. It is reported that in a *Sejm* committee one deputy questioned the Government about the continuing arrest of the Primate, Cardinal Wyszynski.

Addressing the session, Premier Cyrankiewicz noted that it was taking place in an atmosphere of 'unusual enlivenment of political life' and he assured the deputies that this was a lasting transformation. 'I repeat, lasting,' he added, 'because we still very often meet fears . . . that this may be a kind of spring proclaimed arbitrarily . . . and that someone might equally arbitrarily decree its conclusion.' The process of democratization of the political and economic life, said the Premier, was 'irreversible'.

The Kremlin must have been worried by the excessive speed and vigour of this liberalization, that had already gone further than in other Communist countries, and Ochab hastened to reassure the Soviet leaders. In an article published in the Moscow *Pravda* on April 29 he admitted that there was 'ideological instability' in the Polish Party, that the press did publish outright anti-Party criticism, and that there had even been anti-Soviet outbursts, but he assured his readers that the working class knew how to deal with those 'slanderers and opportunists'. According to Ochab, PZPR was engaged in a battle on two fronts: against Stalinism and against 'petit bourgeois waverings and lack of principles, against attempts to undermine Party discipline and the unity of the Party ranks, and in particular against all attempts to undermine the friendship between the Polish and the Soviet peoples'.

The course set by Ochab might have succeeded in a truly Communist country—in Poland it was doomed to failure. Only a small minority of PZPR were true Communists, the bulk of the members having joined for opportunist reasons, and that small minority was now profoundly shaken in its beliefs. An iconoclastic mood was abroad among them and they were not prepared to accept guidance from anyone; the individualistic temperament of the Poles had asserted itself.

On May 1 *Po Prostu* published a long poem by Wiktor Woroszylski, entitled *Questions of a Party Man.*

> The Party is right.
> Are the people at its top
> Also always right?
>
> The Party is the brain of our class.
> Am I
> to have an empty skull?

Woroszylski asked six other similar 'questions', reflecting the mood of young intellectuals, who were savouring their first taste of freedom. The leadership of the Party could fight on the ideological front either with arguments which were not heeded, or by reimposing severe censorship, and this they were unwilling to do. On the other front, however, in the fight against Stalinism, progress could still be made, and there the leadership could gain popular acclaim. On May 7 it was announced that Jakub Berman, the *eminence grise* of the Bierut regime, had resigned from the Politbureau and from his post of Deputy Premier. No explanation was offered, but the public was quick to draw its own conclusions. They remembered that Berman had been responsible for the secret police and for cultural matters, and' it was he who had dismissed the editor of *Nowa Kultura* after the publication of the *Poem for Adults*. To the public mind Berman was the remaining arch-Stalinist and the leaders of the Party must have hoped that his dismissal would convince the people of their sincerity in proclaiming a freer, better and more democratic life. But the people were waiting for deeds, not gestures, and their patience was limited.

4

BLACK THURSDAY AT POZNAN

THE Poznan riots of June 28 should not have taken the régime by surprise. The Government and the Party knew that side by side with the ideological crisis an economic disaster was overtaking the country, and that the workers were in an ugly mood. The outbreak of violence in Poznan that, according to official sources, resulted in fifty-three people being killed and more than three hundred wounded, was a climax of a mounting chorus of protests. But the régime was unwilling or unable to act. As happens so often in a dictatorship, the warning signs were largely ignored and, when the storm came, it seemed like a bolt out of the blue.

During the first six months of 1956 Poland was without an economic plan, an event somewhat unusual in a Communist State; a six-year plan had come to an end on December 31, 1955, and the new five-year plan was not yet ready by mid-summer. It was not the absence of a plan, however, that was causing the economic crisis; it was the collapse of the economy, combined with disagreements among the leaders, that led to delays in the drafting of the new plan. In fact Poland was not suffering from any lack of planning, but from a severe excess of it.

Even Communist economists were saying jokingly that their system had replaced the capitalist discipline in factories and chaos in the markets with chaos in factories and discipline in the markets. Chaos in factories was only one of the causes of the crisis; another was the situation in agriculture.

The Communist leaders themselves had had to admit more than once that there was a 'disproportion' between the development of industrial and agricultural production, a fact hardly surprising since their grandiose plans for a rapid industrialization of the country, particularly in the field of heavy industry, were not matched by a corresponding increase in agricultural output. On the contrary, the Communist policy of forced collectivization, compulsory deliveries and victimization of the independent peasant had led to strong opposition among the rural population and to great inefficiency in the use of the land.

The result was a shortage of food in a country which used to export a great deal of it. This shortage in turn led to high prices, in spite of several price reductions decreed by the Government. People were in fact saying 'God protect us from yet another price reduction'.

The Communist leaders, while admitting some of their shortcomings, tried to hide behind a smokescreen of figures. In February they published the results of the six-year plan and claimed that real wages had increased by 27·6 per cent since 1949.[1] This statement was received by the naive with incredulity and by the critical with derision; the people knew that no such increase in their standard of living had taken place. A careful analysis of the official figures also made nonsense of the claim.

During the years 1949–55 the index of nominal wages rose from 100 to 225·7 and the official index of prices of consumer goods and services rose to 176·7; on the face of it, these figures confirmed the claim that real wages had risen by more than a quarter. The lie was given by a table of prices of thirty-three selected articles that was published at the same time as the results of the plan. Anyone with a pencil and piece of paper could work out that, taking 1949 as a basis, the index of prices of various essential commodities,

[1] *Nowe Drogi* (Warsaw, February 1956).

even on the controlled official market, had risen much more than the index of nominal wages. Here are some of the figures:

Nominal wages	225·7
Potatoes	339
Pork	340
Beef	386
Sugar	228
Coffee	784
Bread	200
Alcohol	250
Coal	262
Galvanized buckets	384

Even if the very large increases of prices of food and coal were compensated by reductions in the prices of manufactured goods, which they were not—among the thirty-three articles listed the only reduction was in the price of radio sets—these figures belied any claim about an increase in real wages. In a poor country, like Poland, food accounts for the bulk of a family's budget, and bread and potatoes play a particularly important part. While the increase in the price of bread was somewhat smaller than the increase in nominal wages, potatoes must have become something of a luxury for the lower paid workers. Moreover, the increases quoted were for prices prevailing on the official market that supplied only a proportion of the population's needs. The index figure for food in this market was given as 211·5, which was just about compatible with the claim about the increase in real wages, but even the Government index of prices on the free market stood at 291, thus contradicting the claim.

A further contradiction was provided by the official consumption figures per head of population, which registered a fall in the consumption of sugar, soap and detergents between 1951 and 1954.

In his speech on April 6 Ochab repeated the claim about

44

increases in the standard of living and announced that from
May 1 the wages of the lowest paid workers would be raised
to 500 *zlotys* a month admitting at the same time that 'it
certainly is not easy to live on 500 *zlotys* either'. Ochab did
not hold out any hopes for an immediate general improvement for the rest of the population because in 1956 it would
be impossible to allocate for the raising of wages 'as many
billions of *zlotys* as is required by the urgent and often acute
needs of workers and peasants'.

The press devoted itself to the description of those 'urgent
and acute' needs of the population and started to search for
the underlying reasons. Some newspapers went so far as to
report the suspicion prevailing among the population that
deliveries to the Soviet Union were responsible for Poland's
misery, but their main attention was directed to the faults of
the system and most of them seemed to agree that too rigid
and too centralized planning was one of the chief causes of
trouble. Even Jerzy Putrament, who was not one of the
'reformists', and was certainly far removed from the 'enraged' critics of the system, came out with an attack on
planning. Writing in the literary review *Przeglad Kulturalny*
on April 5, 1956, he described in vivid terms the adverse
effects of sanctions against non-fulfilment of the plan and
bonuses for over-fulfilment. 'Non-fulfilment of the plan,' he
wrote, 'has become something so terrible that people will do
anything to avoid it. A mason foreman reports artificially
increased results of the work of his gang, as otherwise he will
not gain a bonus. The bookkeeper accepts the return because
he is also interested in avoiding the catastrophe of non-
fulfilment. The director pretends not to notice anything.'

Putrament added that in Poland 'people do not live ex-
clusively on their wages, they do not spend their bonuses on
extras and luxuries', and the system of bonuses has become
'a powerful promoter of public swindling of the State'. He
drew attention to the 'harmfulness of exaggerating the alleged

increase in the standard of living' and asked that people should be told the truth about the economic situation.

This appeal was taken up with gusto by a number of newspapers led by *Po Prostu*. The resulting picture was one of a planner's dream turned into a nightmare.

In the issue of June 10 *Po Prostu* carried three long articles devoted to economic problems and each of them contained a load of dynamite. Under the title 'The problem which does not exist', the newspaper revealed the existence in Poland of unemployment on a serious scale. In spite of all the industrial expansion there were at least 300,000 unemployed, with a concealed unemployment probably several times greater.

In the second article Jerzy Urban (the 'converted cynic', quoted in Chapter 3) described his impressions of a visit to Lodz, Poland's main cotton centre. He found there obsolete machinery, inefficient direction, bad planning, low production, falling productivity and apathy. His conclusions were damning. 'We have created,' he wrote, 'iron principles and rules for our economy, "supreme laws" in the form of plans, "untouchable systems" of managing production, etc. . . . Everybody, from the worker up to the Chairman of the State Planning Commission, knows that something is wrong, but they just shake their heads helplessly, unable to act, unable to break out of the magic circle.'

The third article, entitled *The Price of the Plan*, was devoted to the chaotic conditions in factories as the result of bad and over-centralized planning, combined with the insistence that the plan should be fulfilled irrespective of economic and human considerations. The author described how erratic supplies of materials and bad management led to the workers on the one hand losing their bonuses, and on the other being forced to work fantastic hours to achieve at least a fictitious fulfilment of the plan, which had become more important than the economic welfare of the country. The author wrote:

Twelve times every year the last ten days of each month become a virtual hell of production in many engineering works. . . . Nobody can help it. People are powerless. The avalanche of production rolls on relentlessly, submerging everything. It is the production, which should have taken place during the first twenty days of the month. The Plan is the Law. This slogan becomes full of meaning in every factory on the 20th of each month. This happens not only for ideological reasons, but mainly for material ones. The plan means bonuses. The plan means for many workers the achievement of a minimum standard of living.

While *Po Prostu* reporters were writing their articles, seven hundred Polish economists were attending a congress in Warsaw to discuss the state of the country's economy. Some members of the Government were to report on the results of the six-year plan and describe the principles of the new five-year plan, but at the last moment they cancelled their speeches, perhaps because they knew the mood of their audience. According to reports published in *Trybuna Ludu* (June 6 and 9) the economists were unanimous in complaining about the degradation of their science. One of the most outspoken was Professor Oscar Lange; he said that the oppressive rule of dogma was killing Polish economic thought, which had already been suffering from sterility caused mainly by the lack of access to statistical material. According to Lange 'moral and political appeals and administrative orders had been substituted for economic policies'.

Another speaker, Professor Kurowski, went even further and attributed the weakness of Polish economy to 'the monopoly accorded to one economic school' and spoke of the 'uncritical approach to Soviet science'. This point was developed by several other economists who also stressed the importance of increasing the supply of consumer goods, thus openly contradicting Khrushchev's current policy. Professor

Fabierkiewicz made an even more heretical remark, when he said that the Soviet system suited a country with immense natural resources, but was harmful when applied elsewhere, as was shown by Poland's experience.

After the congress *Po Prostu* (June 24) asked: 'Why has no five-year plan been formally introduced, although half a year has elapsed since the end of the six-year plan? We may be mistaken, but we think that this delay conceals something alarming. . . .'

These articles and speeches provided only a pale reflection of the mood of the population, and especially of the workers. Discontent was growing so rapidly that the Party was forced to act against its better economic judgment. On June 20 Ochab, contradicting his own statement of April 6 that there was no money for raising the wages of any but the lowest paid workers, paid a hurried visit to the coal district of Silesia and personally pacified the miners with a 15 per cent wage increase. This averted trouble in the mines, but probably at the same time increased the discontent among other less privileged workers.

Poznan, the fourth largest city in Poland, was getting restive. The local press had published a number of pungent criticisms of the administration, management of factories and even of the attitude of the Party executives in the larger industrial establishments. A chronic and severe housing shortage combined with a local shortage of bread helped to create an explosive situation.

Nearly 20,000 workers at ZISPO, the largest factory in Poznan, named after Stalin, were seething with discontent. Because of increases of production norms, their average wages had gone down by 3·5 per cent since 1954 and their earnings were further reduced by excessive tax deductions; the workers claimed from the Government the repayment of 11 million *zlotys* which had been illegally deducted from their overtime pay (the official rate of exchange at that time was

11 *zlotys* to the pound, but in purchasing value the equivalent was at the most 100 *zlotys* to the pound).

In section W of ZISPO the workers had even stronger grievances. Bad supplies of components and raw materials made it impossible to fulfil their production norms and they had suffered a severe cut in wages. Similar complaints were voiced by the workers in the Poznan railway repair shop and in other engineering works.

On Saturday, June 23, the workers of ZISPO held a meeting and demanded that a delegation should go to Warsaw to seek satisfaction from the central authorities. The following Monday the workers elected a delegation thirty men strong, which arrived in Warsaw on Tuesday and had talks at the HQ of the Metal Workers' Union and at the Ministry of Machine Industry. None of these moves were given any publicity at the time. According to official statements, made several days later, the talks at the Ministry lasted more than seven hours and the delegates obtained satisfactory promises. The workers had presented five demands but reading between the lines of a broadcast given the following week (July 6) by a member of the delegation, only two of them had been fully met, those relating to the repayment of taxes, and the question of bonuses. In reply to the main demand for a 20 per cent wage increase the delegates obtained only vague assurances that the matter would be reviewed.

There is some mystery as to what happened to the delegation at the end of the Warsaw talks. According to a broadcast by one of the delegates on July 1: 'We all returned to the works on Wednesday morning and there, at 14.00 all the delegates reported back and explained the way matters had been dealt with. On Thursday all the delegates were in the factory and started work in the morning.' On that Wednesday and Thursday, however, Poznan was full of rumours that the delegation had failed to return from Warsaw and that it had been arrested. Dealing with these rumours in a broadcast

49

on July 6 one of the delegates explained that they might have arisen from the fact that the delegation had divided in Warsaw and some members returned to Poznan on a much later train.

Whatever the truth about the fate of the delegation, the ZISPO workers were clearly dissatisfied with the result of the Warsaw talks and on Thursday morning the night and day shifts together decided to stage a demonstration. They formed a procession and started an orderly march towards the city centre, carrying improvised banners and posters: 'We want bread' and 'We want lower prices and higher wages'. The demonstrators were soon joined by workers from other factories and passers by and at ten o'clock a large crowd filled the square in front of the Town Hall. The police were not much in evidence and made no attempt to disperse the demonstrators.

Black Thursday, which was to claim so many victims, began with this peaceful demonstration, but even a perfectly orderly march by the workers must have made a strong emotional impact on the city. Here was the first strike and the first spontaneous manifestation of protest since 1939. Wild rumours swept the city and the crowds in the centre began to grow. In the main square several speakers addressed the demonstrators, including the Propaganda Secretary of the district committee of the Party, who was frequently interrupted.

Gradually the demonstration acquired a political and a revolutionary character. More improvised banners and posters appeared: 'Down with the Russians', 'We want freedom', 'Down with false Communism', 'Down with dictatorship' and 'Down with the Soviet occupation'. Probably acting on the rumour that the ZISPO delegation had been arrested, the crowd attacked the city gaol, freed the inmates and obtained arms from the guards; later the crowd turned against the radio station engaged in jamming Western broadcasts and destroyed it. Not having found the delegates in the gaol the demonstrators attacked the UB (Security Police) building and it was there that the first shots were fired about eleven o'clock.

At this stage the picture becomes much more confusing in spite of the presence of many Western observers who were attending the Poznan International Trade Fair. Any individual has only a very limited field of observation and must rely on hearsay to complete the picture and, as it happened, none of the foreign visitors was in a position to see what exactly did happen outside the UB building. According to official statements the security police fired on the crowd only after Molotov cocktails had been thrown at their building and shots fired from the crowd. On the other hand some observers report that a woman member of the security police, faced by a hostile crowd, lost her head and fired, killing or wounding a woman and a child. There is no doubt that among the early victims were some women and children, and this enraged the crowd still further.

All observers agree that the demonstrators were not organized and did not appear to be acting in accordance with any preconceived plan. The attack on the security police HQ, for instance, was a frontal one, and no attempt was made to surround the building or take it from the rear. One high ranking Communist said later in private that up to the moment of the first shots a couple of fire engines using their hoses could have put an end to the demonstration. The authorities, however, instead of using the fire brigade called in the army.

Two lorries of infantry and three tanks drove up to the centre of the disturbance outside the UB building. They were greeted with cheers from the crowd and shouts 'Poles don't shoot Poles!' Again it is not clear what happened during the next few minutes. One version is that the officer in charge of the infantry was shot by the security police, according to another he was killed by a stray bullet. In any case, soon Polish flags were hoisted on the army lorries and the workers were in possession of the tanks, but they did not know how to use them. The fighting grew more intense and widespread; other public buildings were attacked including police stations, where the demonstrators obtained arms without meeting much resistance.

More and more people were drifting towards the centre of the city. The crowd started to sing religious and patriotic songs, and Polish flags were carried. Elsewhere there was some looting of shops and at least one member of the security police was lynched; overturned trams and cars were used for barricades.

Gradually more troops and tanks arrived on the scene, but only some took part in the fighting. Some witnesses claim that the crews of the tanks which did fire on the crowd were Russian (this is doubtful, as there was no Soviet garrison in Poznan, only some technical troops), and many people were convinced that the Soviet army had been called in; many of them also believed that the fighting in the city was a part of a nation wide insurrection and that the workers in other major cities had also risen in arms.

It took a considerable military force to bring the situation under control; by the evening the army was in occupation of the centre of Poznan. Sporadic firing continued throughout the night and the following day, but it was localized and apparently no one was hurt; on the morning of Friday, while the centre of the city resembled a battlefield, the International Fair was open as usual.

From the point of view of the Party the events of the Black Thursday were a disaster. They showed conclusively that the workers were bitter and ready to fight, that the population was solidly against the regime, the Party organization was ineffective and bankrupt, the army at least partly and the uniformed civil police (the militia) wholly unreliable.

Because of the large number of foreign visitors in the city there was no hope of suppressing the news of the Poznan riots and the Government was forced to make a prompt announcement. At 8.30 p.m. a communiqué was broadcast by Warsaw radio announcing 'serious disturbances' and blaming 'imperialist agents and the reactionary underground' for exploiting economic difficulties and the grievances of the population. Thus from the beginning Polish propaganda developed the twin theme of dissatisfaction among the workers, which admittedly was justified, and the alleged work of foreign agents who were fishing in the troubled waters and stirring up disturbances directed against the 'people's regime'. Gradually, however, more and more attention was paid to the economic causes of the riots and less and less to the provocation theory. *Trybuna Ludu*, for instance, wrote on July 6: 'The strike action of Poznan workers—and this basic and painful truth must not be concealed or embellished—was to a considerable extent caused by bureaucratic distortions of the proletarian State.' The main lesson of Black Thursday, according to this official newspaper, was the necessity 'to turn from words to deeds in our economy'.

These accents of truthfulness in Poland were in contrast with the line adopted by the Communist Party of the Soviet Union. A resolution of the Central Committee of the CPSU on June 30 spoke of the large sums of money assigned by 'American monopoly capital for increasing subversive activities in Socialist countries' and asserted that 'the anti-popular riots in Poznan have been paid for from this source'. The Soviet resolution also affirmed that 'the working people of Poznan resisted the hostile actions and provocations'.

The Russians stuck to this line, while the Poles were departing from it further and further. For the first time there was an open split between Moscow and Warsaw.

Much more important than the debate on the responsibility for the riots was the question which was on everybody's lips: what effect will the outbreak have on the policy of the Party? Premier Cyrankiewicz, who had hurried to Poznan on hearing of the riots, gave a preliminary answer when he broadcast from the city the following day. He uttered a sharp warning that anyone who makes an attempt to weaken 'the people's power' will be crushed, but at the same time he appealed for still more criticism of 'our work, our mistakes and shortcomings' and he gave an assurance that 'the bloody events in Poznan will not stop or weaken the efforts of the Party and Government aimed at the democratization of our life'.

This was a reassuring statement, but it came from an ex-Socialist Premier, and not from the chief of the Party. Did it represent the view of the Politbureau, and in particular of Ochab, that 'good and tough Bolshevik'? The answer to this question was to be given at the forthcoming VII Plenum of the Central Committee of PZPR. Other points on the agenda of this important meeting were the new five-year plan and the bankruptcy of the Party organization in Poznan demonstrated by the events of Black Thursday.

5

THE STRUGGLE BEHIND
THE SCENES

MEETINGS of the Central Committees of the various Communist parties are almost like a parody of a Synod of a church. The High Priest (the First Secretary) opens with a review of the situation and formulates the 'key tasks of the Party'. His speech is usually very long and overwhelms the listeners with a mass of detail and copious statistics. Though delivered in secret (even the fact that the meeting is taking place is often not announced at the time) the High Priest's speech, or at least such parts as are considered suitable for profane ears, is broadcast and widely publicized in the press. Occasionally other key speeches by members of the Politbureau are also published, but the discussion is (or at least used to be) invariably secret. After the meeting is over the decisions of the Synod are usually announced and they form a part of the Communist canon until the next Plenary session of the Central Committee, or Plenum for short. These decisions are always a faithful reflection of the High Priest's opening speech.

The political life of Communist run countries is supposed to be divided into neat chapters, each opening with one Plenum and ending with the next. Only very occasionally the Party Congress is summoned, and this provides a special landmark, the end of the volume. After the Congress, the numbering of the successive Plenary sessions of the Central Committee starts afresh from one, and the new volume of Communist history begins. Congresses of the Communist

Party of the Soviet Union are, of course, particularly important landmarks.

In July 1956, when the VII Plenum of the PZPR was due to meet, it was clear that important decisions had to be taken regarding the policy of 'democratization', which had been formally adopted at the III Plenum in January 1955, but not applied with any vigour until after the VI Plenum in March 1956 when Edward Ochab succeeded the late Boleslaw Bierut to the post of First Secretary. Now the Party had three months' experience of 'democratization', and this experience included the revolt of the intellectuals against the Party and the Poznan riots. The time had come for a reassessment.

There is a story, which circulated in Warsaw cafés where politicians and journalists meet, that having reluctantly accepted the office of First Secretary, Ochab turned to Khrushchev, who was present at the VI Plenum, and asked for advice about the best way to carry out his new duties. 'Make yourself popular,' was allegedly the terse reply of the Soviet leader.

Whether this story is true or not, Ochab certainly followed a policy which should have gained him some measure of popularity. He relaxed the censorship of the press, allowing a freedom of discussion without parallel in a Communist country; he removed from the Politbureau and from the Government the men who had been associated with the worst excesses of Stalinism; he raised the wages of the lowest paid workers and he began to address the nation in an adult and relatively honest language. Yet, if the aim was to increase his own popularity or that of the Party, Ochab's policy resulted in a resounding failure.

Rightly or wrongly Ochab was regarded as a Stalinist and people suspected that he was introducing the reforms against his better judgment, yielding to pressure from below. In any case the reforms did not and could not go far enough to satisfy the masses, who were demanding a higher standard of living, real independence from Russia, freedom for the Church and real political democracy. Considering the pent up hatred of the regime any relaxation of the dictatorship seemed to be courting disaster.

After the Poznan riots the advocates of repressive measures, the reactionary wing in the Party, could argue that disaster was in fact overtaking the Communist regime as the result of 'democratization'. But could the clock be put back, could the regime of terror be reintroduced, without causing a violent explosion? If not, how could the Party survive the growing wave of criticism and open discontent? These were the questions, which the VII Plenum, summoned to Warsaw for July 18, had to answer.

Before the meeting the 'progressives' in the Party leadership made their views public. The daily *Trybuna Ludu*, which at that time was edited by Jerzy Morawski, one of the secretaries of the Party, endorsed Premier Cyrankiewicz's analysis of the Poznan riots, adding that the outburst would not have taken place if 'economic democratization' had kept pace with 'political democratization'. Even more outspoken and far reaching were the views of Professor Oscar Lange, one of the leading economists and a member of the Central Committee.

On the eve of the Plenum, Lange published an article (*Życie Gospodarcze*, July 13, 1956), which received wide publicity on the radio and in the press. It contained a powerful indictment of the existing economic system and a plan of reform. Lange admitted that the six-year plan, by not raising the standard of living, had failed 'in the sphere which constituted the social justification of building socialism', while the continued use of methods of compulsion was 'leading to the disintegration of the national economy'.

According to Professor Lange the new five-year plan, even though it would bring an improvement in the standard of living, would be insufficient and too slow, and 'if the process of disintegration of the national economy continues, the fulfilment of the plan will be doubtful'. Having thus painted a gloomy, but fully justified picture of the current crisis, Professor Lange outlined an emergency economic plan that was 'also a political necessity', because people did no longer believe in the possibility of overcoming the current crisis.

Lange's emergency programme contained a great deal of common sense economics, but relatively little Marxism, and it has turned out to be a document of some importance, for three months later Gomulka more or less adopted it as his policy. Lange wanted immediate and drastic steps to increase the supplies of food and consumer goods. This was to be achieved by mobilizing all existing resources, including even those of the defence industry, and by increasing imports of consumer goods and fertilizers, while cutting exports of food. The workers were to be given an interest in production by having a share in the management, while individual peasants, small private firms and craftsmen were to be encouraged and helped instead of being persecuted. Finally, according to Lange, capital investment was to be used to obtain further increases in the supply of consumer goods, fertilizers and raw materials.

Would this plan, so far removed from orthodox Marxism, meet with the approval of the Central Committee? The decision of the Plenum was awaited with unusual interest, and the duration of the session—it lasted ten days, instead of the customary two or three—was an indication of the disagreements within the Party's leadership.

Ochab's opening speech would have caused a sensation a few months previously, but in the conditions prevailing in July it sounded inadequate. As far as it went, his analysis of past mistakes of the Party was correct and the future programme of action was sound, but not far reaching enough.

The first part of Ochab's speech was devoted to the Poznan riots. The First Secretary said:

In the appraisal of the reasons of these incidents, it would be erroneous to concentrate attention above all on the machinations of *provocateurs* and imperialist agents; it is necessary to look first of all for the social roots of these incidents, which have become a warning signal for the Party, testifying to the existence of serious disturbances in the relations between the Party and various sections of the working class.

According to Ochab the social roots of the riots were to be found in the 'highly insufficient' rise in living standards during the six-year plan. He admitted that the efforts of the Party to improve matters were 'not energetic enough and not always consistent' and as a result 'a conviction arose in the broad sections of the population that the Party and the Government had not done everything in their power to help the workers and employees in their difficult material situation'.

Having thus roundly condemned his own Party, Ochab went on to examine past mistakes in some detail. He put a great deal of blame on 'bureaucratic distortions' which resulted in callousness and indifference in the Party and Trade Unions towards the population, and this in turn led to the 'loss of contact with the masses'. The grievances of the Poznan workers were justified, and so were 'the serious doubts' raised by the official calculations of increases in real wages during the six-year plan period. Ochab disclosed that a special commission of the Central Committee had estimated that the increase in real wages was in fact less than half of the 27·6 per cent given earlier in the year and even this reduced estimate did not apply to all the workers, as there were groups whose situation had 'somewhat worsened'.

Turning to the future, Ochab declared that the new five-year plan 'must increase the average real wage of workers and the average income of working peasants by 30 per cent', but when this is achieved 'the level of wages will still be relatively low'. However, to increase wages any faster would mean inflation, 'it would mean fooling the workers, giving them alleged rises, which in reality correspond with a fall in the standard of living'.

In agriculture Ochab foreshadowed a better deal for individual farmers, who should not all be branded as *Kulaks*, this term being reserved only for those who were 'constantly exploiting' hired labour. He also announced proposals for abolishing the compulsory deliveries of milk, a measure that would be popular with the peasants.

On the question of democratization Ochab was most explicit: 'It must be emphatically stressed that the Poznan incidents cannot constitute any justification for any attempt whatsoever to turn back the process of democratization'. Further steps would be taken in that direction in the political and in the economic field. Echoing Lange, Ochab said that the workers must be given a direct interest in the management of their enterprises by the expansion of the functions of works councils. He also announced that the draconic law on labour discipline, dating back to the days of Stalin, would be abolished.

Respect for the rights of the citizen and the need for safeguards against the recurrence of past excesses of the secret police, was the next point in Ochab's speech, and then followed a somewhat puzzling reference to the need to combat not only nationalism, but also anti-Semitism.

Finally Ochab announced the official line on public criticism. This was serving a constructive purpose, though it was marred by irresponsible outbursts. In the future the freedom to criticize would not mean 'freedom for any criticism' for 'we do not want criticism from the position of the enemy and we shall not allow such criticism'.

Ochab was followed by Premier Cyrankiewicz, who delivered a report on the principles of the new five-year plan.

The Premier's political remarks were fully in tune with those of the First Secretary, while in the economic sphere Cyrankiewicz elaborated in greater detail what Ochab had said and also announced a two-year emergency programme designed to remove 'the most painful grievances of the working masses', another echo of Professor Lange's article published before the Plenum.

While the Plenum was still in progress Marshal Bulganin, accompanied by Marshal Zhukov, arrived in Warsaw, ostensibly to attend the National Day celebrations on July 22. Normally this would have been an occasion for yet another platitudinous speech on Polish-Soviet friendship and the solidarity of the peace-loving socialist camp. This time, however, Marshal Bulganin must have felt the need for an open intervention into Poland's internal affairs. In a speech he made on the eve of the celebrations he said that the Poznan riots had been caused by hostile agents and showed the need for 'a high level of political vigilance, a persevering struggle against shortcomings, a consistent improvement in the work of the State apparatus . . . and a decisive strengthening of the organs of the dictatorship of the proletariat'.

Bulganin also attacked the 'hostile and opportunist elements' that were exploiting the struggle against the cult of the individual by publishing 'wrong interpretations in the columns of certain periodicals in socialist countries, including Poland'. He sounded a warning: 'we cannot close our eyes to the attempts at weakening the international bonds of the socialist camp under the label of so-called "national peculiarity", or to the attempts at undermining the power of people's democratic countries under the label of an alleged "broadening of democracy".'

Marshal Bulganin clearly spoke a different language from Ochab and Cyrankiewicz. What he said sounded like a directive to the Plenum, that was to resume its session after the National Day celebrations. The Soviet guests were tactfully dispatched on a tour of Poland (which incidentally did not include a visit to Poznan), and while Marshal Bulganin was making speeches about Polish-Soviet friendship, the Plenum continued its deliberations.

There is no published record of the debates, but there have been so many deliberate leaks and so many public references to the various speeches that we have quite a good picture of what did take place behind the closed doors of the Central Committee. Judging by all the accounts, it was an exceptionally lively meeting and the heated discussions reflected the uneasy mood of the Party. There were demands from the floor that those responsible for the crimes and the blunders of the Stalinist period should be punished, and not just allowed to retire in peace; there were insistent proposals that the rehabilitation of Gomulka and his associates should be completed by readmitting them not only to the Party, but also to their rightful place in the Party hierarchy; there were speeches attacking the Soviet Union in scarcely veiled terms; there were repeated demands that the Politbureau should resign.

The main debate, however, was about the policy of democratization and this revealed a deep division among the leaders of the Party. The chief spokesman of the reactionary wing was Zenon Nowak, a member of the Politbureau and one of the First Vice-Premiers, who hitherto had been regarded as a moderate. He launched a strong attack on all the critics of the Soviet Union, singling out the intellectuals who came under special censure; he advocated the abandonment of further democratization, and recommended the old policy of the stick and the carrot. The stick was to take the form of suppression of criticism, while the Party would seek greater popularity by holding out the carrot of substantial wage increases, far in excess of those envisaged by Ochab. Even if this resulted in inflation, Nowak thought it a risk worth taking because, in the short run, it would stop the rot and rally the workers behind the Party. To gain still greater popularity, Nowak wanted the Party to limit the number of Jews in leading positions, thus courting the favour of the anti-Semitic sections of the population.

There was no room for compromise between the policies outlined by Ochab and by Nowak. After prolonged and passionate arguments it became clear that the reactionaries were in a minority. This was demonstrated by the result of the elections for the Politbureau to fill vacancies created by the death of Bierut and the 'resignations' of Berman and Radkiewicz. Two of the new members of the Politbureau, Adam Rapacki (the Foreign Minister, an ex-Socialist and a close associate of the Premier) and Edward Gierek (one of the Party's secretaries), were regarded as progressives and one, Roman Nowak (who should not be confused with Zenon Nowak), occupied a middle-of-the-road position.

In the end the reactionaries, not wishing to create a split, voted for resolutions that followed the policy outlined by Ochab and Cyrankiewicz, and the decisions of the VII Plenum were unanimous.

In the economic field the VII Plenum proclaimed a policy somewhat similar to Lenin's NEP. Encouragement was promised to the independent farmer and artisan, a system of material incentives was to be introduced in industry and agriculture, State industry was to adopt business accounting and its administration was to be decentralized. The new five-year plan was to increase the average real wages and the income of the rural population by 30 per cent, with even greater increases for the lowest paid workers, while a special housing drive was to produce 1,200,000 additional rooms by 1961.

The political resolution asserted that 'all tendencies to hamper democratization owing to the Poznan events would be erroneous and politically harmful'. A greater role was to be assigned to the *Sejm* (Parliament), which was to exercise a more effective control over the activities of the Government.

Free discussion would be encouraged inside the Party, but it would have to keep within the general Party line. Finally, the VII Plenum decreed the end of discrimination against members of former underground organizations, who had become 'loyal citizens'.

The resolutions of the VII Plenum ignored Bulganin's directive and chartered a course towards further liberalization. This programme, however, was destined to remain a dead letter for some months to come; the reactionary group, though forced to vote for the resolutions, was still strong enough in the Politbureau to prevent the necessary reforms.

The exact composition of the two opposing groups did not crystallize for some time, for there were several waverers. The reactionary faction, which later became known as the Natolin group (after a suburb of Warsaw where a club for the Communist *élite* is situated), was composed of four members of the Politbureau, Zenon Nowak, Franciszek Mazur, Jozwiak-Witold, and Marshal Rokossovsky; it also included the chairman of the TUC, Klosiewicz, and the Deputy Minister of Defence, General Witaszewski. The progressives were led by Premier Cyrankiewicz, the Politbureau members Rapacki, Gierek and the First Secretary, Ochab, who after some hesitation joined the group some time during the summer; also out of the six secretaries of the Central Committee, five were in favour of further liberalization.

Two members of the Politbureau, Alexander Zawadzki (the Chairman of the State Council and nominal Head of State) and Roman Zambrowski, both of whom later joined the progressives, occupied at that time a somewhat ambiguous position.

Realizing that Gomulka was the only Communist leader who enjoyed the confidence of the rank and file of the Party and the respect of the nation, both the progressive and the reactionary factions were trying to enlist his support. The first approach to Gomulka came apparently from the Natolin group; the well-informed special correspondent of *Le Monde*[1] reported that already in May, on the advice of the Soviet Ambassador Ponomarenko, Gomulka had been invited to join the Politbureau. It is obvious why this offer was made: Gomulka would lend some of his personal popularity to the compromised leadership, while remaining the prisoner of the Natolin group, which at that time still had the majority in the Politbureau.

Gomulka declined the invitation; he did not want to re-join the leadership through the back door and have his hands tied. It was rumoured that he insisted on becoming the First Secretary and wanted to be elected to that office by the Party Congress, which was due to meet in the spring of 1957.

After the VII Plenum a delegation of the Central Committee, led by Ochab, went to see Gomulka to discuss his return to the Party. On August 4 came a brief announcement that the talks had taken place and that Gomulka had been readmitted to the Party. Two friends of Gomulka were restored to Party membership at the same time; one of them, Zenon Kliszko, who had been expelled together with Gomulka, was now given the post of Vice-Minister of Justice, while the other, General Marian Spychalski, a former Minister of Defence, remained for the time being out of office.

It seems probable that already in July or August at least some of the 'progressives' came to the conclusion that only Gomulka's return to power could save the Party and the country from a catastrophe; but the forces opposed to Gomulka's return on his own terms were formidable; the Natolin group, through Rokossovsky, was in command of the armed forces, and it enjoyed the support of the Soviet Union. Careful and extensive preparations were needed before the change could be affected. They began in the greatest secrecy

[1] Philippe Ben, *La Pologne de Gomulka*, *Le Monde* (Paris, November 21, 1956).

after the end of the VII Plenum. The only outward sign, which few observers recognized at the time, was a terse communiqué from the Prime Minister's office, announcing on August 24 the appointment of a new commander of the Internal Security Corps: General Waclaw Komar, the recently rehabilitated associate of Gomulka. His control over the well-armed military detachments of the Security Corps proved of crucial importance during the dramatic days of October.

6

THERE COULD BE JUSTICE

On a small hill above the industrial and market town of Czestochowa, rise the walls of a Pauline monastery surrounded by ancient battlements. Within is a small chapel, with the famous picture of the Black Madonna, attributed to St Luke. It has been there since the fourteenth century, attracting pilgrims from far and wide, for this is the national shrine of Poland. The name of the hill, known to every Polish child, is Jasna Gora, the Bright Mountain.

Towards the end of August 1956 Czestochowa was the scene of the greatest pilgrimage in its long history and of a manifestation without precedent in any Communist run country; more than one million faithful people from all parts of Poland assembled there to pay homage to Our Lady of Czestochowa. It was a double occasion: the climax of the Polish celebrations of the Marian year, and the three hundredth anniversary of the proclamation of the Virgin Mary as the 'Queen of the Polish Crown'. The pilgrimage was thus not only a purely religious, but also a national demonstration and, in the special conditions prevailing at the time, it had a deep political significance.

The anniversary the pilgrims were celebrating recalls one of those dramatic twists in which Polish history abounds. In 1655, when King John Casimir was involved in a war against the Russians and the Cossacks, Poland was invaded by a powerful Swedish army under Charles X. Within a few months almost the whole country was in Swedish hands and only a few cities and strongholds were resisting the invader,

67

among them was the fortified monastery of Jasna Gora. It was defended by seventy monks and fewer than two hundred soldiers led by Prior Kordecki. After several weeks of siege the Swedes, in spite of great numerical superiority, had to give up and withdraw. The news of Prior Kordecki's heroic defence swept the country and imbued the nation with a new spirit. Soon the tide of the war turned dramatically and in 1656 King John Casimir, in thanksgiving, dedicated the country to the Virgin Mary.

This then was the anniversary, which Polish Catholics were celebrating in August 1956. The news of the forthcoming pilgrimage spread mainly by word of mouth, for the press gave it no publicity; even the so-called Catholic papers, under the control of the Communist sponsored PAX movement, preserved a complete silence. The Communist authorities, however, behaved with good sense; when they realized the size of the pilgrimage, not only did they refrain from making any difficulties, but they even provided special trains to transport the faithful and arranged for additional supplies of food to Czestochowa, so that the immense crowd would not go hungry.

By August 26 the number of pilgrims at Jasna Gora exceeded one million; some observers put it as high as a million and a half. The monastery became an island surrounded by a veritable sea of people, who filled the adjacent parkland and the avenue leading from the town. High on the ancient ramparts a magnificent procession carried the Byzantine picture of the Black Madonna round the monastery walls and placed it on an altar. The Mass was relayed by loudspeakers to the multitude, who joined in the prayers. By the altar there was an empty throne with a bunch of white and red roses (Poland's national colours)—a silent but eloquent allusion to the absence of the imprisoned Primate, Cardinal Wyszynski.

The huge congregation was addressed by the Bishop of

Lodz, who renewed King John Casimir's vows and consecrated to the Virgin Mary 'every Polish heart and home'. From the sea of kneeling pilgrims, like a mighty wave, came the response: 'Queen of Poland, we promise'.

Here was an overwhelming demonstration of the attachment of the people to their religion; the Communist leaders could not fail to contrast it with the bankruptcy of their own creed. They did not, however, draw the logical conclusion and stop the war against the Church.

During August and September the Communist leadership was fully engaged in their internal struggle and, with a divided Politbureau, no major political initiative was possible. Both the reactionary and the progressive factions were trying to consolidate their positions before it came to the now unavoidable showdown. Members of the Central Committee were addressing innumerable meetings of the Party, giving often conflicting accounts of what had taken place during the VII Plenum, while some of the leaders were seeking inspiration in Moscow and Peking. Of the many comings and goings during that period Ochab's visit to China in September was, perhaps, of the greatest importance, as it may have influenced the First Secretary's future course of action; it also marked the beginning of what looks like a Polish-Chinese axis.

All these moves were naturally veiled in secrecy, as were the negotiations with Gomulka, but the open revolt of the intellectuals continued and the whole country was in a state of tension and confusion. 'Where are we? Whither are we going?' asked a poet describing the uneasiness of the people who were 'in a delirium of impossible possibilities'.[1] Another poet, Julian Przybos, had no such doubts. In answer to an invitation by *Nowa Kultura* to discuss the work of the Association of Writers, he said quite bluntly: 'Complete freedom, limited only by the social conscience of the artist, is the con-

[1] Anna Kamienska, *Disquiet, Nowa Kultura* (Warsaw, August 26, 1956).

dition of artistic creation. . . . Freedom under socialism must not be more limited than in a bourgeois society, and the freedom of literature should be greater.'[1] Several other writers expressed similar views.

An economist, Edward Lipinski also writing in *Nowa Kultura*[2] (which together with *Po Prostu* had become the vanguard of the revolution), proclaimed open heresy and suffered no ill consequences. He wrote:

Neither Marx nor Lenin created a complete theory of Socialist economy and they did not analyse the conditions which ensure the successful operation of stimuli and incentives to progress, growth and development. . . . If planning is centralized, this leads eventually to the omnipotence of bureaucracy and to political autocracy. . . . The nationalization of land does not bring us one step nearer to Socialism. . . . Our state farms . . . have become a negation of Socialist economy and a crying example of the inferiority of pseudo-Socialist economy, when compared with capitalism.

The reactionary wing of the Party was worried by this frank speech, which was attacking some of their most cherished dogmas. Behind the scenes they tried to limit the freedom of the press, but they were rebuffed by Premier Cyrankiewicz. Opening the autumn session of the *Sejm* on September 5 he said:

The discussion in the press and press criticism have contributed in a very great measure to the advancement of the democratization of our country. In the course of this discussion and criticism the press has committed quite a few mistakes, but nothing can erase the great effort, which has brought the replacement of ossified embellishing propaganda by live, bold, creative criticism, and a participation in the shaping of political thought in Poland. Certain circles, however, are trying, on the pretext of combating and rejecting the errors committed by the press, to condemn the press as a whole. This, of course, is . . . undoubtedly in conflict with the idea of democratization.

[1] *Nowa Kultura* (Warsaw, September 2, 1956).
[2] September 9, 1956.

Describing the policy decisions of the VII Plenum, Cyran-kiewicz outlined the future role of the *Sejm*, which should concern itself with the control of the administration and the making of laws, instead of merely endorsing them. The Government would limit the number of decrees and would present proposals for legislation in good time, thus allowing for a critical examination by the *Sejm*. The Premier also said that he attached great importance to deputies' questions being answered promptly and exhaustively.

Several deputies took up this theme and the most out-spoken intervention was by Professor Julian Hochfeld of PZPR, an ex-colleague of the Premier in the Polish Socialist Party before its merger with the Communists. He criticized the Government for not allowing the *Sejm* to discuss the Poznan riots and he went on to analyse the position of parliament in a Communist State. Hochfeld agreed with the Premier, that the *Sejm* should control the executive, but he pointed out the difficulty arising out of the Party's 'specific leading position in the system of the dictatorship of the proletariat'. In his view the crux of the process of demo-cratization was not so much in the replacing of unitary leadership by a collective one, as in countering autocratic leadership by creating an elected, responsible and con-trolled leadership, which would be subject to recall.

This was probably the first instance in any Communist country of one of the essential principles of parliamentary democracy being seriously put forward by a member of the Party. It was even more surprising that Professor Hochfeld's views should be given wide publicity in the press and on the radio.

While the *Sejm* was not allowed to discuss Poznan, it was told by the Premier about the impending trials. 'I can assure the House,' said Cyrankiewicz, 'that both the investigation of the Poznan incidents and the court proceedings themselves are and will be in keeping with the strictest requirements of the rule of law and legality. The trials, of course, will be public.'

The task of the Prosecutor-General was not made easy by this insistence on the rule of law and legality and by the political complications of the case, especially by the official admission that the workers of Poznan did have legitimate grievances, which had since been settled at a considerable cost to the treasury. Black Thursday had been followed by mass arrests; three weeks after the riots 323 persons were officially stated still to be under arrest and in September that number was reduced to 154, against whom indictments had to be prepared.

The Poznan trials were awaited with great interest, for they would provide answers to a good many important questions: did the Government and the Party really mean what they had been saying about the respect for the rights of the citizens and the need for the rule of law? Would the charges and the trial be of a political or criminal nature? Would an attempt be made to prove the foreign provocation theory?

Soon after the first two trials opened on September 27 it became quite clear that a fundamental change was indeed taking place in Poland, and that all the talk about freedom, legality and democratization was not just propaganda. From the beginning the prosecution made a clear distinction between the workers who had gone on strike and staged a peaceful demonstration, and those who during the riots committed criminal acts, such as murdering security policemen, using firearms or looting. Nobody was prosecuted just for taking part in the strike or demonstration, and no one was accused of being a foreign agent.

At the very opening of one of the trials the prosecutor stated that some of the suspects had been brutally treated by the police and confessions extracted from them. He withdrew the evidence obtained under duress and announced that the responsible senior police officers in Poznan had been dismissed; criminal proceedings would be instituted against those guilty of acts of brutality.

The next surprise was the behaviour of the counsel for the defence, who, for the first time in eight years were allowed to put up a genuine fight in the interests of the accused, instead of just pleading guilty and asking for extenuating circumstances to be taken into consideration. The presiding judges did not try to hamper the defence and gave an impression of impartiality. The results were unexpected; in several cases the defence managed to turn the tables on the prosecution and put the Communist regime in the dock. They achieved this by various means, including the testimony of expert witnesses, one of whom gave evidence on the psychological and social significance of the riots. He was Professor Chalasinski, a sociologist of Lodz University, and his testimony is worth summarizing.

The crowd, which gathered outside the Poznan castle, said Professor Chalasinski, exercised great psychological influence on the people assembled there. It was a demonstration against wrongs, accompanied by an almost religious atmosphere, typical of the singing of religious songs or the national anthem. The effect was particularly strong, as it was the first demonstration of this kind—an illegal demonstration in People's Poland, and for many thousands of the people present, the first demonstration in their life. Against this psychological background the first shots occurred before noon, followed by rumours that public security officials were shooting at children. These rumours, said Professor Chalasinski, no doubt brought back the memory of the crowd to the acts of lawlessness and brutal practices of the public security organs in the preceding period. In this atmosphere normal people must have experienced a powerful feeling of moral outrage. The action of the crowd against the officers of the public security, concluded the witness, was the consequence of the moral outrage at cruelty and not an attack on an office of State.

Even the prosecutors themselves could not avoid dwelling on the 'mistakes' of the authorities. One of them, Prosecutor Lehmann, concluding his case against three youths accused of taking part in the murder of a security policeman, said: 'Criminals must be brought to trial and punished. But by punishing them, no one will absolve those, who through ill-will and negligence, through divorce from the masses, and through lack of responsibility, helped to create a situation which, in so tragic a manner, reflected the discontent prevailing among the working people of Poznan.' According to the prosecutor, however, a clear distinction had to be made between the working class and the hooligans who were in the dock. He demanded that the accused should be punished severely as this 'will be understood as the fulfilment of the requirements not only of law but, above all, of morality'.

The defence, and in particular counsel Hejmowski, were able to demolish this argument with great effect. You cannot order young people to lead moral lives and expect results, he said. The accused had been brought up during the war and the following period of the 'breaches of legality', when moral brakes had been removed. They had ceased to respect the authority of State, parents, church or school, but whose fault was it? It was the fault of the older generation, which had lost the respect of the youth and created the abnormal conditions of amorality.

Hejmowski also disagreed with the distinction between workers and hooligans, which the prosecution tried to make. Hooligans, he said, were not a social class. There were only acts of hooliganism and it was nonsense to say that hooligans could not belong to the working class. When the workers of Poznan demonstrated in the streets, to draw attention to their just demands, they were accompanied by young people, for youth is always the dynamic force of any demonstration against authority.

The following eloquent plea was made by another counsel for the defence:

From this tremendous social movement, which involved tens of thousands of people, the prosecution has selected certain fragments and a number of individuals, and now asks that these people should be convicted for the offences they may have committed. The dividing line is provided by the law: we do not try people for their participation in the strike, but we shall try those who have committed offences. But were only these people guilty of breaking the law? Thousands of people on that day infringed the penal code.

The defence counsel enumerated the various offences committed by the demonstrators by leaving their work and taking part in an unlawful assembly, which led to acts of violence, and he asked:

Where is the dividing line between these thousands of offenders and the handful of men who have appeared in court? I know very well why all those people have not been brought to trial; the right principle, the only just principle in this case, the principle of *nolle prosequi* has been applied. The prosecution and the judiciary have understood that we had to deal with a mass movement, that it was not the individuals, but the crowd that had committed all these offences.

The same principle of no prosecution, he argued, should also be applied to the men in the dock, and if indulgence had been shown to the bureaucrats responsible for the dissatisfaction among the workers, it should also be shown towards the accused.

A third defence lawyer described an incident during the riots when a boy seized the Polish flag from the hands of a woman demonstrator who had fallen, and held it high amid the shooting. Addressing the court the counsel said:

I speak with respect of that boy. What happened here in Poznan on June 28 has become a chapter in our history. That which was

75

beautiful will live on in our nation for ever; that which was wrong will not. I believe that the blood of the victims did not flow in vain.

In another of the Poznan trials one of the counsel recalled the famous painting by Delacroix, which shows the spirit of freedom leading the masses in the 1830 revolution, and said:

If the police of Charles X had won that battle, the prosecutor of that time would have dragged those young people into the court and said that they were hooligans and criminal elements; but, since the revolution did win, they are regarded as national heroes and their picture has become a symbol of revolution.

The sentences were remarkably lenient if one considers the gravity of the charges. For instance, two of the youths, accused of killing a corporal of the security police, were sentenced to four and a half years, and the third to four years' imprisonment, the court having accepted the argument of the defence that they had attacked their victim, not because he was a member of the security police, but because they thought that he had killed a woman and a child.

Altogether, of the 154 people awaiting trial in September, only thirty-seven appeared in courts on various charges, mainly that of looting. Two were acquitted, four had their sentences of imprisonment suspended, twenty-three went to prison for terms varying from six months to six years and the trial of the remaining eight was adjourned before the even more dramatic events of the second part of October replaced Poznan as the centre of attention.[1]

[1] An official communique published in the Poznan newspaper *Glos Wielkopolski* on November 4 announced that the Public Prosecutor had decided not to proceed against those still awaiting trial because 'among other things . . . the situation which arose on June 28 was to a great extent a consequence of the errors and distortions of the past era, and of the incorrect behaviour of certain authorities. The atmosphere prevailing on June 28 has greatly influenced the action of the participants in these incidents'.

Later, all those already sentenced were released, with the exception of the three youths who had been accused of murdering a security policeman, but their sentence was to be reviewed.

There can be no doubt that during the Poznan trials the authorities allowed justice to take its course disregarding the likely political consequences. Also no restrictions were placed on the reporting of the trial by foreign journalists, and eminent lawyers from the West were allowed to be present. On the other hand, the reporting of the proceedings inside the country was not completely free and one of the local newspapers in Poznan announced that, though it sent its own reporters to the trial, it had, for reasons beyond its control, to carry the official news agency account of a speech by one of the defending counsel. Nevertheless, enough was published in the Polish press and broadcast on the radio to enable the population to see that the age of terror was past and that there could be justice.

PART II

REVOLUTION

7

PLOT—COUNTERPLOT

AT the beginning of October 1956, the two opposing factions of the Communist leadership in the deepest secrecy were putting finishing touches to their plans of action. The progressives, led by Premier Cyrankiewicz and the First Secretary of the Party, Ochab, were getting ready for the return to power of Wladyslaw Gomulka, with a programme of further democratization and independence from Moscow; the reactionaries of the Natolin group were trying to frustrate the changes, to maintain the closest ties with the Soviet Union and to return to the tough Communist line.

One day we shall perhaps know the full story of both conspiracies, but at the time of writing only fragmentary and circumstantial evidence is available; even so it has the making of a first-class thriller. Resisting, however, any temptation to introduce fictional embellishments, here is a straightforward account of what is known of the plot and counterplot.

Some time in the spring or summer the progressives in the Polish Politbureau came to the conclusion that the only policy which could rally support among the population, without at the same time provoking a Soviet intervention, was a more pragmatic form of Communism which took into account national characteristics and susceptibilities. In Poland, Communism had to allow a large measure of personal freedom, it had to make peace with the Catholic Church, recognize the peasant's desire to own his land, and produce at least an appearance of independence from Moscow. Asked if all this meant a Polish brand of 'Titoism' one of the Polish Communists said: 'Not at all. If you look upon the Kremlin as the Vatican, Tito represents the High Church of England, while we are the non-conformists.'

The 'non-conformists' needed a leader, and the only personality sufficiently respected in the country was Wladyslaw Gomulka. Many secret talks took place between him and various members of the Politbureau. Gomulka's terms were stiff: he was to become the First Secretary of the Party, a new Politbureau had to be elected, composed of men who agreed with his policy, and Marshal Rokossovsky, the symbol of Soviet domination, had to be excluded from it.

It is not certain at what stage Ochab agreed to these terms and made up his mind to resign in favour of Gomulka, but this probably happened soon after the VII Plenum. It seems that Ochab, an honest and not very ambitious man, was not keen to carry the burden of leading the Party and was reluctant to accept the office of First Secretary after the death of Bierut. It did not take him long to realize the seriousness of the situation, but for some time he hesitated as to which course to choose. Even after he had decided to support Gomulka many outside observers thought that he still belonged to the Natolin group.

Thus, some weeks before the October events, two of the three key men in Poland were working for the return of Gomulka—Cyrankiewicz, who headed the Government, and Ochab, who headed the Party.

They knew, however, that the forces opposed to Gomulka's policy were not to be trifled with. The Natolin group was very strong within the Politbureau and within the Government, while the Soviet nominee, Marshal Rokossovsky, was in command of the army, ably assisted by his Stalinist deputy, General Witaszewski, and a large number of Russian officers. Also there were at least three Soviet divisions in Poland and overwhelming Russian forces all round her frontiers.

The only military formations which did not come under

Soviet command were the troops of the Internal Security Corps, and these were in August placed by Cyrankiewicz under General Komar, who had been victimized during the Stalinist purges and who was a supporter of Gomulka. At the same time considerable undercover activity went on within the Polish army, with the aim of at least neutralizing it in the event of a showdown but, not surprisingly, no information on this subject has come out of Poland.

On the other hand, we know much more of the underground political activities of the progressives, especially in Warsaw, where the metropolitan Committee of the Party was controlled by them and where the workers of the *Zeran* motor-car factory were particularly active. The fullest account to reach the West was an emotional, and at times confused, report by a shipyard delegate from Gdansk who, on his return from Warsaw, addressed a public meeting; a recording of his speech was broadcast by Gdansk radio on October 26. The delegate reported:

The comrade from *Zeran* yesterday described to us in detail the entire period since the XX Congress [of the Soviet Party]. He described the whole road taken by the Warsaw organization and, in particular, by *Zeran* in the battle against the backward forces, which have made their nest in our Central Committee and Polit-bureau. . . . When the entire nation awaited enthusiastically the VII Plenum, when the nation demanded that this Plenum should map out the further road forward, terrible things started to happen. *Zeran* workers have been in contact the whole time with the progressive section of the Central Committee and with some Ministers. They met them secretly in private houses. *Zeran* was followed by the entire Warsaw working class. The comrades from *Zeran* and the progressive part of the Central Committee had their men everywhere, but so did the Natolin group.

Similar talks and secret meetings were taking place in all the major Polish cities. Everywhere the workers were organizing themselves in readiness to support Gomulka and many university students were also preparing to lend a hand in the planned revolution against Stalinism.

The Natolin group were not idle either. Their men were firmly entrenched within the Party apparatus, especially in the provinces; most of the Communist bureaucrats saw their own jobs threatened by the policy of democratization, and decided to support the reactionaries. At thousands of meetings all over the country, spokesmen of the Natolin group addressed workers, trying to set them against the intellectuals by sowing class hatred and by exploiting anti-Semitism, while the progressives addressed similar meetings and did not mince their words about the reactionaries.

In the Politbureau itself the progressives were gaining an upper hand; they could count on about half of the votes and the secretariat was almost solidly behind them. Gradually the waverers came out on their side and the progressives obtained the majority within the Politbureau. By October 9 they were strong enough to force the resignation of Hilary Minc from the Politbureau and from the post of First Deputy Premier in charge of economic affairs. During the Stalinist period Minc had been the economic dictator of Poland, but in more recent times a severe illness prevented him from exercising anything like his former influence. But his resignation at that particular moment was highly significant in the light of Gomulka's known dislike of him. The public assumed that this was a prelude to major changes and some Western correspondents in Warsaw confidently predicted Gomulka's return to power.

The departure of Minc reduced the Natolin group in the Politbureau to four men: Zenon Nowak, Marshal Rokossovsky, Franciszek Jozwiak-Witold and Franciszek Mazur. The first three were also in the Government as Deputy Premiers, while Mazur occupied the not very important position of Deputy Chairman of the Council of State. Earlier in the year Mazur had been reported as the leader of the

Natolin group, but some time in the summer he disappeared from the scene and was reputed to have gone to live in the Soviet Union, a move not altogether surprising in view of his strong ties with Moscow. Mazur was in fact the only old Bolshevik in the Politbureau (he had taken part in the October revolution of 1917) and it was rumoured that even his Natolin colleagues did not trust him completely.

By October 15 the progressives were ready. The following communiqué was broadcast by Warsaw radio that evening:

Today, a session of the Political Bureau of the PZPR Central Committee took place and was devoted to preparations for the VIII Plenum . . . which will be convened on October 19. Taking part in the session of the Political Bureau was Wladyslaw Gomulka.

At that meeting, the progressives revealed their plans: Gomulka was to become the First Secretary of the Party, a new Politbureau was to be elected, with only nine members instead of thirteen, and it was not to include Marshal Rokossovsky or any other member of the Natolin group. In fact only five members of the old Politbureau were to retain their seats. It is hardly surprising that these proposals were not accepted with the customary unanimity; probably they obtained the support of the majority only because some of the members, who were being deprived of their seats, realized the gravity of the situation and decided to put national considerations above personal ambition.

Defeated in the Politbureau, the Natolin group did not give up the struggle. What communications passed between its members and the Soviet Embassy or Moscow we do not know, but it is reported that the Soviet Ambassador in Warsaw, Ponomarenko, called on Ochab and conveyed to him on Khrushchev's behalf an urgent invitation to visit Moscow in the company of all the members of the Politbureau and of Gomulka. The invitation was declined.

Probably the Soviet leaders had already reconciled them-

G

selves with the idea of Gomulka's return to power, but they were exceedingly worried about the proposal to remove Marshal Rokossovsky from the Politbureau, as this implied to their minds Poland's break away from the Soviet bloc. The other members of the Natolin group also seemed more concerned about the position of the Marshal than about their own political future. In fact the question of Rokossovsky's membership of the Politbureau became the major issue.

With only four days to go before the meeting of the Plenum the Natolin group put into operation their plan for a military *coup d'état*, which must have been prepared in close consultation with the Russians. Sinister movements of troops began; Rokossovsky's Polish army and Soviet units stationed in Poland started to move towards Warsaw and other major cities; some Soviet formations were reported to be crossing into Poland from East Prussia and Germany, where a significant regrouping of Russian forces was taking place; Soviet warships suddenly appeared in strength off the Polish coast and maintained a vigil within sight of the ports of Gdynia and Gdansk.

The Natolin group had also ready a black list of seven hundred leading progressives, including Gomulka, a number of Ministers and members of the Central Committee who were to be arrested on the eve of the Plenum, leaving the country in the hands of Rokossovsky and his pro-Soviet allies. According to the report by the shipyard delegate broadcast by Gdansk radio, the seven hundred progressives were to be arrested by the army, and the operation was timed to last only one hour.

Somehow the progressives learned of this plot and were ready with their counter-measures. General Komar's Internal Security Corps occupied all key buildings in the capital and provided guards for those threatened with arrest. Large units of the Corps were placed in positions commanding all the approaches to Warsaw and were given orders not to allow army formations to enter the city. At the same time the loyal workers and students were mobilized, and some of them were armed.

Two days before the Plenum was due to meet the Natolin group issued a public warning, using a somewhat unusual channel, perhaps the only one left to them; *Slowo Powszechne*, the pseudo-Catholic newspaper of Boleslaw Piasecki, carried on October 17 an article, in which the following passage attracted attention:

> . . . in the present situation the possibility of governing Poland depends on setting a limit to this discussion . . . otherwise we shall provoke, instead of democratization, the necessity for a brutal implementation of the *raison d'etat*, in circumstances similar to martial law.

Far from stopping the discussion about democratization, this warning only served to increase still further the public demand for sweeping reforms and the popular hostility towards the Natolin group. All over the country meetings were held demanding more democratization and the return of Gomulka. In Warsaw not only at *Zeran* but also in a number of other factories, at the University and at the Polytechnic mass meetings expressed themselves forcibly in favour of Gomulka, and against the reactionaries; there were even demonstrations in the streets. This movement gathered crescendo as the meeting of the Plenum approached, and by the morning of October 19 a truly revolutionary atmosphere reigned in Warsaw and several major cities.

When the decisive hour struck the Natolin group found that they could not count on any popular support, that the secret police and the Internal Security Corps were solidly behind Gomulka and his associates. The only weapon left to the reactionaries was the army: commanded by Rokossovsky and his Soviet generals it would surely tip the scales in their favour. But when orders came from the high command, they were not obeyed by Polish officers and soldiers. The rank and file of the army was also behind Gomulka.

To quote once more from the report by the shipyard delegate from Gdansk:

> Suspicious troop movements started now, and again *Zeran* workers, who have many vehicles at their disposal, sent comrades to places practically all over Poland, so that the progressive forces in the Central Committee knew all about these troop movements. What attitude the troops adopted, you all know. When orders were issued to staff and political officers, they answered simply that these orders would be ignored. They said that they were with the people and they would defend the working class.

The patient preparatory work of the progressives paid rich dividends. The plot of the Natolin group was stillborn, and only an open military intervention by the Soviet Union itself could change the course of events in Poland. But was that intervention necessary and desirable? The Soviet leaders decided to see for themselves. Early in the morning of October 19, before the meeting of the VIII Plenum, the most powerful delegation ever sent abroad by the Soviet Communist Party arrived uninvited and unannounced at Warsaw airport; it was composed of Khrushchev, Kaganovich, Mikoyan and Molotov. The Soviet leaders were showing signs of violent temper; October 19 promised to be a stormy day in Poland's history.

8

THE DAY OF DECISION

THE skies were grey over Warsaw and a thin rain was falling, as the members of the Central Committee were assembling for the VIII Plenum. In spite of outward calm the city was tense; everyone knew that this was the day of decision, the Central Committee was to elect new leaders and adopt a new programme, but only very few realized that before this could happen another and an even more dramatic decision had to be taken.

At ten o'clock First Secretary Ochab opened the proceedings of the Plenum. There was no rhetoric in his speech and no striving for effect, but his first sentences caused a minor sensation:

Dear Comrades, the agenda of this Plenum of our Central Committee told you that I would report on some of the problems facing our Party. The situation which developed in the leadership during the last period prevented me from preparing this report in time. As you have already received the draft resolutions, approved by the Politbureau, I shall limit myself in this introduction to a report on the latest decisions of the Politbureau.[1]

Ochab announced briefly that the Politbureau would move the co-optation to the Central Committee of Gomulka and three of his associates, Spychalski, Loga-Sowinski and Kliszko, that they were proposing to limit the number of members of the future Politbureau to nine so as to 'ensure

[1] This and subsequent quotations are taken from the report of the proceedings of the VIII Plenum published in *Nowe Drogi* (Warsaw, October 1956).

89

unity', and were putting forward the name of Wladyslaw Gomulka for the post of First Secretary. Though not unexpected, these proposals were sensational enough, but they were followed by a virtual bombshell:

I would also like to inform you, Comrades, that a delegation of the Presidium of the Central Committee of the CPSU, composed of Comrades Khrushchev, Kaganovich, Mikoyan and Molotov arrived in Warsaw this morning. The delegation wishes to conduct talks with our Politbureau.

Ochab proposed that, after Gomulka and his three associates had been co-opted, the proceedings of the Plenum should be suspended until 6 p.m. Most of the members of the Central Committee seemed to be stunned by the news of the arrival of the formidable Soviet delegation, but one woman member inquired innocently why was the adjournment necessary.

'It arises out of the necessity to conduct talks with the delegation of the Presidium of the CPSU, which is already in Warsaw', was Ochab's curt reply. Some members wanted to know who would be talking to the Russians, and Ochab explained that the Polish delegation would consist of members of the Politbureau, who would be accompanied by Gomulka. From the floor came the motion that a new Politbureau should be elected before the talks with the Russians. This was opposed by Ochab who, before putting it to the vote, appealed to members for a 'sense of responsibility'. The motion was lost, Gomulka and his friends were readmitted to the Central Committee, the Politbureau and Gomulka were empowered to conduct talks with the Soviet delegation, and within half an hour the session was suspended.

Gomulka, Cyrankiewicz, Ochab, Rokossovsky and all the other members and deputy members of the Politbureau, with the mysterious exception of Franciszek Mazur, went to the Belvedere Palace, where the meeting with the Russians began immediately.

At 6 p.m. the Central Committee resumed its session to hear a brief report from Ochab:

I would like to inform you, Comrades, that conversations between our Politbureau and the Soviet delegation, which were conducted in a down to earth atmosphere, have lasted several hours. They concern the most fundamental problems of the relations between our countries and our Parties, as well as the development of the situation in Poland which causes a deep anxiety among our Soviet comrades. As our Soviet comrades somewhat unexpectedly had to take the decision to fly to Warsaw and they are anxious to return as soon as possible, we would like to continue our talks tonight and the Politbureau suggests that the Plenum be adjourned till tomorrow morning.

Back to the Belvedere Palace, for further talks with the Russians. These lasted for several more hours and it was late at night before a communiqué gave the first official news of the presence of the Soviet delegation in Warsaw and of the discussions it had with the Politbureau. The talks, said the announcement, had dealt with 'current problems of interest to both Parties', and had been conducted 'in an atmosphere of Party and friendly sincerity'. The communiqué ended with the announcement that in the immediate future a delegation of the Polish Politbureau would visit Moscow in order to discuss 'the further deepening of political and economic co-operation between Poland and the Soviet Union, as well as the further strengthening of fraternal friendship and co-operation between the PZPR and the CPSU'. Another communiqué, the following morning, announced that the Soviet delegation had departed at 6.40 a.m. That was all the Polish people were at first told about the historic discussions with the Russians, and as so often is the case with Communist announcements, the Warsaw communiqué concealed much more than it said.

What did in fact take place in the elegant eighteenth century Palace of Belvedere on that Friday, October 19, 1956?

The Central Committee, when they met next morning at eleven o'clock, heard a report by Alexander Zawadzki. This revealed more than the uninformative communiqué. Zawadzki said:

Our Soviet comrades gave as the reason for their sudden arrival and for the composition of their delegation, which is known to you, the deep anxiety of the Presidium of CC of the CPSU regarding the development of the situation in Poland. They told us that, together with us, they wanted to clarify the direction in which this situation would develop and to discover our point of view. They were particularly worried by the development of all forms of anti-Soviet propaganda and the lack of reaction or insufficient reaction to that propaganda on our part.

The Russian visitors were also interested in our proposals for the composition of the leadership, which will emerge from the VIII Plenum. They pointed out that the proposed membership was known everywhere but, in spite of our ties, we had not informed our Soviet comrades of our plans. Generally, one of the shortcomings in our recent relations, we were told, was a lack of sufficient contacts between us and an insufficient supply from our leadership of direct, authoritative information about the situation in Poland. I would like to say, however, that from the beginning to the end the question of the composition of our future leadership was discussed as an internal matter of our Party and its Central Committee.

Having made this somewhat self-contradictory statement Zawadzki said that the discussions had been marked by outbursts of temper on both sides, but added innocently that it was with 'the best intentions to clarify fundamental problems'. He went on:

We tried to reassure our Soviet comrades regarding our intentions and our proposed action, and also about our internal situation and the mutual relations between People's Poland and the Soviet Union. We tried to explain to the comrades the process of democratization which is taking place here, its meaning and its irreversible nature. We pointed out that the main task of the Plenum was to ensure that the Party and its leadership should head this movement and guide it. . . . We agreed with the Soviet comrades that contacts between us were insufficient and that many things today may cause their anxiety. We pointed out that the bad symptoms here are a scum on the wave of a good and creative process, that they are in the nature of shortcomings and distortions, which we shall be able to liquidate, and direct the purified process of democratization, provided that after this Plenum . . . we succeed in improving the leadership of the Party and regain what has been lost in the past period, as far as the position of the Party is concerned and the relations between the Party, the working class and the nation.

Finally, referring to the communiqué on the talks, Zawadzki drew special attention to the announcement about the forthcoming visit of the Polish leaders to Moscow, and added:

It is the intention of all of us that, in accordance with the traditions of the revolutionary movement, the relations between our Parties and our countries, even though they might have suffered here and there, should be straightened out and should develop in the direction of still closer friendship and co-operation, in the interest of both our countries.

If the published record of the proceedings of the Plenum is complete, and there are reasons to believe that it had been subject only to some slight 'editing', the members of the Central Committee were not told much more about the conversations with the Russians. During the subsequent discussion, except for a passing reference in Cyrankiewicz's speech, only Ochab added a little to the picture. He described the talks as 'sincere, difficult and bitter' and spoke of the 'baseless and unheard of accusations' by the Soviet leaders. He confirmed that the Polish press came under special attack:

The Soviet comrades made the bitter charge that even in a bourgeois country, for instance in Finland, it would be unthinkable for the press to print such accusations and libels of the Soviet Union, which percolate sometimes, and that not so very rarely, to the pages of our press, the press of a friendly country.

That is all the Polish participants in the dramatic talks of October 19 were prepared to say and the Russians have disclosed nothing. Warsaw, however, was at that time full of Western correspondents who were allowed to send their reports without any hindrance from the censor. Some of their dispatches were very circumstantial and entertaining, but they must be regarded with some caution; the correspondents, of course, were not allowed to attend the meetings between the Soviet leaders and the Poles, they were not even allowed at the airport for the arrival and departure of Khrushchev and company. By the nature of things they could report only what they themselves saw, which was little, what they read in the Polish press, which on this occasion was next to nothing, and what their Polish contacts were willing to tell them, which was not necessarily accurate. For instance, most correspondents reported that in addition to Khrushchev, Mikoyan, Kaganovich and Molotov, also Marshal Zhukov, accompanied by a posse of Soviet Generals, had arrived in Warsaw. This was, in fact, not true; Marshal Zhukov was at that time in the Soviet Union.

By comparing the press reports with the disclosures at the VIII Plenum, and particularly by reading between the lines of Zawadzki's speech, one can however piece together a picture of what really did happen between the Poles and the Russians during that decisive Friday, October 19.

The Russians were in a raging temper; Zawadzki has admitted that much. On arrival, Khrushchev shouted angrily at the Polish leaders: 'We have shed our blood to liberate this country, and now you want to hand it over to the Americans, but in this you will not succeed, this will not happen!' Allegedly he refused to shake hands with the Poles, called them 'traitors', and accused them of having plotted with the Americans 'and the Zionists' to get Poland out of the Soviet bloc.

On noticing Gomulka, Khrushchev turned to the Soviet Ambassador, Ponomarenko, with the question: 'And who is that?' Before the Ambassador had a chance to reply, Gomulka answered in Polish: 'I am Gomulka, whom you kept in prison for three years.'[1]

The report of this exchange comes from a well-informed correspondent, who points out that Gomulka and Khrushchev did not know each other (when Gomulka was in power before 1948, Khrushchev occupied a relatively minor position in the Soviet hierarchy). Now the irresistible force of Khrushchev's fury was meeting for the first time the immovable object of Gomulka's determination. The discussions promised to be lively.

The Soviet position, as stated by Khrushchev, was quite simple. What the Poles described as democratization looked to him suspiciously like anarchy, which would lead to the downfall of Communism in Poland. The disintegration of the Communist system had to be stopped; the press had to be brought under control, popular demands resisted and any sign of opposition stamped out. This was not the time for sweeping changes in the leadership of the Party. If the Poles wanted to have Gomulka and one or two of his friends in the Politbureau, they could please themselves, but the trusted men of Moscow, and in particular Marshal Rokossovsky, must remain. To remove them would mean Poland breaking away from the Soviet bloc and this the Russians could not tolerate. If necessary, they would use force.

On the Polish side most of the talking was apparently done by Ochab. He shared the Russian's anxiety about Poland's internal situation, but his diagnosis and proposed treatment were diametrically opposed to Khrushchev's. Indeed the situation was threatening to get out of hand, and

[1] Reported by Philippe Ben in *Le Monde* (Paris, November 22, 1956).

should repressive measures be taken they would only pre-
cipitate a revolt. The Party, instead of suppressing the spontaneous movement towards democracy, must put itself at its
head, guide it and eventually control it. Any other solution
would mean courting disaster. To be successful, however, the
Party must be led by someone free from the Stalinist stigma,
who would be trusted by the people. The people must also
see that this man is really in control. In any case, the composition of the Politbureau was a Polish internal matter. If
the Russians really wanted to avoid a blood bath and keep
Poland in their camp, they should allow Polish Communists
to settle their own affairs in the full knowledge of prevailing
circumstances.

Neither side would budge from its position and an acri-
monious discussion ranged far and wide. By the late evening
no progress had been made and the talks looked like ending
in deadlock. At the last moment the Russians appeared to
give way; Khrushchev, suddenly all smiles, assured the Poles
that it was entirely up to them whom they elected to their
Politbureau. Why this *volte-face*? It is reported that Gomulka
threatened to broadcast to the Polish nation and tell the
truth about the Soviet demands. This may have affected the
Soviet decision, but the crucial factor must have been the
military situation.

In view of the defiant attitude of Ochab and Gomulka, no
doubt supported by Cyrankiewicz and many others, the
Russians realized that only military force could bring the
Poles to heel. When Khrushchev landed in Warsaw on
Friday morning he must have thought that if the Poles did
not yield to threats it would be a relatively simple matter to
achieve what he wanted by military means. By the evening
he learnt from Rokossovsky that this was not the case. The
Marshal had by that time received reports showing that his
Polish troops could not be relied upon to carry out his orders
and that in case of a showdown with the Russians they would

in fact fight against the Soviet troops. Khrushchev was also told by the Poles of the disposition of General Komar's Internal Security Corps. It all added up to the conclusion that the only way to impose Soviet will on the Poles was by throwing Russian troops into action. The outcome would not be in doubt; but before the Poles could be subdued the Russians would have to fight a bloody war and this Khrushchev and his colleagues were not prepared to do at that moment. They decided to play a waiting game.

The Poles were told to get on with their Plenum, leaving further discussion till the following week, when they in turn would visit Moscow. The uninformative and friendly, but not too friendly, communiqué was issued and the uninvited Soviet guests went to the airport. There were smiles and handshakes before the Russians boarded their plane. The Poles had won the day, but the movement of Soviet forces continued.

9

GOMULKA SPEAKS

THE Central Committee resumed its session at eleven o'clock
on the morning of Saturday, October 20. Only a few hours
had elapsed since the departure of the Soviet aircraft which
was carrying Khrushchev and his colleagues back from their
sudden visit to Warsaw. The implications of the Soviet intervention were becoming clear to the people, and workers and
students in Warsaw were coming out into the streets to
demonstrate their support for Gomulka. The Soviet troops
in Poland were still poised for action.

The seventy-five members of the Central Committee
watched intently as Wladyslaw Gomulka mounted the
rostrum for the first time in seven years. Prison and illness
had aged him; the lines on his face were chiselled more
deeply, his scant hair was turning grey, but his eyes were as
bright as ever, and those eyes could burn with fury. Would
he lash out against his persecutors? Would he remind his
listeners that most of them, too, must bear a share of responsibility for his imprisonment? They knew that he could
be fierce and ruthless; they had thrown him out and now they
had asked him to come back and to save them. What would
he say? Many of those present must have awaited Gomulka's
speech with anxiety.

When I addressed the November Plenum . . . seven years ago
I thought that it was my last speech to the members of the Central
Committee. Seven years have elapsed since that time . . . these
years are a closed chapter of history. I am deeply convinced that
that period belongs to the irrevocable past. There has been much

evil in those years. The legacy of that period, inherited by the Party, the working class and the nation in many spheres is more then alarming.

These dignified opening words seemed to indicate that it was not Gomulka's intention to dwell too much on the past, that he would concentrate on the present and the future. Some of his listeners were no doubt reassured, especially when Gomulka turned immediately to the decisions of the VII Plenum. His readmission to the Party, he said, had been made conditional on his acceptance of the decisions of that Plenum. This acceptance was not unqualified:

I have certain reservations about the resolutions of the VII Plenum. . . . They concern the appraisal of the past, as well as the Party's policy in the field of agriculture. Apart from this I consider these resolutions to be correct. . . . Much more important, however, than the adoption of the resolutions and their acceptance is that these decisions should be put into practice.

Gomulka's reservations regarding the evaluation of the past turned out to be very wide indeed. He started with the economic side:

The resolutions of the VII Plenum deal with the achievements and errors of the six-year plan. The great expansion during that period of the productive capacity of our industry, particularly the heavy industry, is described as the most important result, which overshadows everything else.

Without trying to belittle that achievement, Gomulka pointed out that even in the industrial sphere not everything was well. It was claimed, for instance, that the output of coal had gone up by more than 20 million tons. But how was this increase obtained? In 1955 the miners worked more than 92 million hours of overtime. The productivity of labour had in fact fallen by more than 12 per cent since 1949 and by 36 per cent since before the war. To make up for it the miners had been forced to work on Sundays, thus endangering their health, and the employment of soldiers and prison inmates in the collieries had become a part of the system.

Gomulka went on:

Here, comrades, is another example. At the cost of tremendous investments we have built a motor-car factory at *Zeran*. A new industrial establishment has risen, an establishment which, at a disproportionately high cost, produces only insignificant numbers of cars of an old type, very heavy on petrol, a type which is probably not made anywhere else in the world. Can the construction of an establishment of this kind be called a contribution to the productive capacity of our industry?

Gomulka next turned to wider economic issues:

Generally speaking, after the conclusion of the six-year plan, which according to its promises was to raise high the standard of living of the working class, we are now faced . . . with immense economic difficulties which grow from day to day.

He criticized the inefficient use made of investment credits from abroad. Everyone present knew that this was a direct attack on Poland's former economic dictator, Hilary Minc, though Gomulka did not mention him by name. It was also a veiled attack on the Soviet Union which had imposed on Poland much of the detailed economic planning, was the main provider of credits, and also the main supplier of capital goods. 'Until this very day,' said Gomulka, 'machinery and equipment ordered for various projects, which have long since been struck out from plans, continue to arrive.' The result? An adverse balance of payments and inflation. 'The Central Committee,' added Gomulka with reproach, 'did not even muster up the courage to draw the necessary Party consequences with regard to those responsible for this state of affairs.'

The agricultural policy of forced collectivization came next under Gomulka's fire. It was a policy which led to smaller returns for greater investment, and even leaving political considerations aside, it was a policy of failure. To prove his

5. *a*. Conference between Chou En-Lai and the Polish political leaders.

5. *b*. One of the Poznan trials opens.

6. *a*. Cyrankiewicz and Gomulka.

6. *b*. Gomulka being greeted in Moscow by Bulganin and Khrushchev.

contention Gomulka produced a wealth of figures which for the first time showed Communist agriculture in its true light. His figures can be most conveniently presented in the form of a table:

Type of Farm	% of Land	% of Total Production	% of Livestock Production	Value of Output per Hectare	
				zlotys	%
Private	78·8	83·9	91	621	100·0
Collective	8·6	7·7	4	517	83·3
State	12·6	8·4	5	393	62·8

Thus the output of State farms, the pride of Communist agriculture, per unit of land was 37·2 per cent lower than that of individual farms, and co-operative farms also came out badly by comparison with those privately owned. And yet, added Gomulka, the State and co-operative farms had received large subsidies and credits, while the individual farmers received none.

Turning to housing in the countryside, Gomulka estimated that the six-year plan, far from improving housing, failed to make up for the annual wastage of old houses, and left the rural population with at least 600,000 fewer habitable rooms. He said:

We must ask ourselves the question, how are we going to solve our overwhelming problems, what to do and where to start, so as to overcome all the difficulties and move forward along an increasingly smoother road? We will have to change a great deal in the methods we have used to date, if we are to reach this goal. The key to the surmounting of our accumulated difficulties is in the hands of the working class. Everything depends on its attitude. . . . Recently, the working class gave the Party leadership and the Government a painful lesson. The Poznan workers used the strike weapon and came out to demonstrate in the streets on that Black

Thursday in June and exclaimed in a powerful voice: 'That's enough! This cannot go on! We must turn back from the false path!'

What were the lessons of Poznan? 'First of all,' said Gomulka, 'the working class has never used strikes as a weapon in the battle for its rights in a light-hearted manner.' If they did strike in Poznan, it was for a good reason, 'they were protesting against the evil which had spread widely in our social system and which has affected them in a painful manner, they were protesting against distortions of the fundamental principle of socialism, which remains their ideal.' With great emphasis Gomulka said: 'The working class is our class, our invincible might. . . . Without it, without the confidence of the working class, each of us would represent nothing but himself.'

Gomulka contemptuously dismissed the foreign provocation theory to which the Kremlin has been wedded:

The attempt to present the painful tragedy of Poznan as the work of imperialist agents and provocateurs was a great political *naïveté*. Agents and provocateurs can exist and be active everywhere and all the time, but never and nowhere can they determine the attitude of the working class. Comrades, the causes of the Poznan tragedy and of the deep dissatisfaction of the entire working class lie within us, in the Party leadership and in the Government.

He described in vivid terms the awakening which had started in the spring of 1956, following the 20th Congress of the CPSU.

A reviving and healthy current has stirred the Party masses, the working class and the entire community. People started to straighten their shoulders. Silent, enslaved minds began to shake off the poisonous fumes of deceit, falsehood, duplicity. The creative and living word began to oust the cliché. . . . On occasion a false note could also be heard, but it was not that note which dictated the tune. The criticism of the past came in a broad wave. It was the criticism of violence, distortions and errors which affected every single sector of life. . . . Above all the working people demanded that the whole truth should be told to them openly, and without any half truths.

At that time it was imperative to 'act swiftly and with consistency, to draw conclusions from the past, to go to the masses with a raised visor, to tell them the whole truth'. The leadership of the Party failed to do it. Gomulka said:

It is impossible to escape from the truth. If one is hiding it, the truth emerges in the form of a dangerous spectre which haunts, worries, revolts and turns insane. The Party leadership became afraid of it. Some were afraid of the responsibility for the bad results of their policy, others were more attached to their comfortable arm-chairs than to the working class which had put them there, others still, and they were the most numerous, were afraid that the working class may not understand the most profound essence of the truth, which they were demanding from their representatives. . . .

Here, then, was Gomulka's condemnation of the past. He had not minced words about the evil of Stalinism and the errors of the Polish Communist leadership, but there was no personal vindictiveness in his speech. He continued:

The ruling of the country demands that the working class and the toiling masses should have faith in their representatives at the helm of state power. This is the moral basis of discharging power on behalf of the working masses. That faith can be continually extended, only provided that the obligations undertaken are fulfilled. The loss of confidence on the part of the working class spells the loss of the moral basis for the holding of power. It is still possible to rule the country under such conditions, but it will be a bad rule.

The working class was able to withdraw its confidence from certain men. That is normal. It is also normal that such men should leave their posts. However, to alter all the bad traits of our life, to lead our economy out of its present condition, it is not enough to change some men, though this may be easy. In order

103

to remove from our political and economic life all the layers accumulated through years, which hamper its development, it is necessary to change a great deal in our system of people's power, in the organization of our industry in the methods of work of the Party and the Government. In brief, it is necessary to exchange all the bad parts of our model of socialism, replacing them by better parts, to perfect this model by using the best existing examples and by introducing into it our own improvements. And this is much more difficult. It requires time, work and courage coupled with wisdom.

But was there time? Gomulka reminded his listeners of 'the impatience of the working classes, resulting chiefly from their living conditions. These in turn are closely connected with our economic situation. Even Solomon could not pour anything out of an empty vessel'.

This being the situation, Gomulka felt that the working class had to be told the painful truth that no increases in wages were possible without corresponding increases of production. He added:

I am unable to give any concrete answer to the question when it will be possible to save further resources for the stepping up of the living standard of the working class. This depends primarily on two factors: in the first place on an improvement in the management of industry and in the entire national economy, and in the second place on the workers, that is on an increase of productivity and on the lowering of output costs.

Gomulka then spoke of the problem of improving the management of industry and the proposed introduction of workers' self-government. He saw no ready answers and was opposed to sweeping changes bringing in untried solutions; instead he suggested experiments in order to discover the respective merits and shortcomings of various forms of workers' self-government, because 'every new mechanism must undergo tests, for as a rule it has various faults and drawbacks'. He also favoured experiments with various forms of material incentives for workers. On one point he was emphatic; whatever the system, it was essential to introduce a realistic method of costing and pricing. The workers and the administration of enterprises simply must know the real cost of all the elements of production and forget the erroneous theory that in socialist economy the law of value does not operate.

Turning to private enterprise, Gomulka saw an important role for the independent artisan; he promised that the persecution of the artisans by means of supplementary and arbitrary tax assessments would stop. He then elaborated his plan for agriculture. Here his programme became even less Marxist. He would abolish all subsidies for co-operative farms. The healthy co-operatives would be given investment credits, but those running at a loss would not be helped and 'members of such co-operatives should be asked if the co-operative should be dissolved'.

The future development of agricultural co-operatives should be guided by the following rules:

(1) Peasants should join the co-operatives voluntarily, without any pressure whatsoever.

(2) The co-operatives to be absolutely independent.

(3) The co-operatives to be entitled to buy all the machines they might need (this would break the present monopoly of State machine stations).

(4) The State would provide the necessary investment credits, give the co-operatives priority in contracts for the supply of the most profitable produce, priority in deliveries of fertilizers and other help.

'If, as a result of the abolition of various forms of grants, which I am proposing, the development of producer co-operation is slowed down, then in my opinion we shall lose nothing either from the economic or from the political point of view,' said Gomulka, and he stressed with great emphasis

his faith in the development of rural co-operatives. He added,
however:

The setting up of producer co-operatives calls for creative, progressive thought, of which no party and no man can hold the
monopoly. In the field of raising producer co-operatives to a
higher level, in the field of searching for and applying the best
forms of co-operation, there is a wide scope for rivalry between
our Party and the Peasant Party, as well as among all those who
strive for the strengthening of the socialist system, the system of
social justice. Why, for instance, shouldn't the progressive Catholic movement compete with us, both in the search for forms of
producer co-operation and in their application? It is a poor idea
that socialism can be built only by Communists, only by people
professing a materialistic social ideology.

This was a refreshing note to hear at a Communist Party
meeting. Refreshing, too, was Gomulka's point that 'the
quantitative development of producer co-operation cannot
be planned because, if the entry into co-operatives is voluntary, planning it would amount to the planning of human
consciousness, and that is impossible'. He went on to condemn
the assumption that 'socialism in the countryside can be built
on the basis of misery and the decline of peasant's holdings',
and spoke with contempt of 'the dogmatic minds' which had
been responsible for agricultural policy. One of the consequences of that policy was the ruin of many of the more
prosperous farmers, and the country was paying for it with
expensive imports of grain. The victimization of the individual farmer would have to stop and the system of compulsory
deliveries of agricultural produce would be abolished as soon
as possible. 'Diverse forms of the production community,' declared Gomulka, 'this is our Polish road to socialism in the
countryside.'

The phrase about 'the Polish road to socialism' became the
slogan of the October revolution. Gomulka had a great deal
to say on this subject:

Even a theory of socialism evolved in the best possible way at any given time, in any given conditions, cannot embrace all the details of life, which is richer than theory. What is immutable in socialism can be reduced to the abolition of the exploitation of man by man. The roads leading to this goal can be and are different. They are determined by various circumstances of time and place. The model of socialism can also vary. It can be such as that created in the Soviet Union, it can be shaped in the manner we observe in Yugoslavia, it can be different still.

Having thus made his declaration of independence of thought, Gomulka proceeded to deal with the relations between Parties and States belonging to the 'camp of socialism'. He said:

These relations ought to be based on mutual confidence and equality of rights, on mutual assistance, on mutual friendly criticism, if such becomes a necessity, on wise solutions, arising out of the spirit of friendship and socialism, of all questions under dispute. Within the framework of such relations every country ought to have complete independence and freedom, and the right of every nation to rule itself in a sovereign manner in its own independent country ought to be fully and mutually respected. This is how it ought to be and, I should say, how it is beginning to be.

Was Gomulka stating a fact or just expressing a hope? There is every reason to believe that it was the latter; the possibility of an armed Soviet intervention was still in balance and he had to choose his words carefully. Having declared his independence, Gomulka hastened to stress the need for maintaining Polish-Soviet friendship.

The Party and all the people, who saw the evil that existed in the past and who sincerely desire to remove all that is left of that evil in our life today in order to strengthen the foundations of our system, should give a determined rebuff to all the whisperings and all the voices which strive to weaken our friendship with the Soviet Union. If in the past not everything in the relations between our Party and the CPSU and between Poland and the Soviet Union was shaping as we thought it should—today this belongs to the irrevocable past. If there are still problems to be settled, this should be done in a friendly and calm manner. . . . And if there is anyone who thinks that it is possible to kindle anti-Soviet moods in Poland, then he is deeply mistaken. We shall not allow the vital interests of the Polish State and the cause of building socialism in Poland to be harmed.

Here, of course, Gomulka was telling only half the truth. He was warning the nation in a slightly roundabout way that there was a limitation to Poland's independence—she had to be friendly to the Soviet Union, in order to survive.

The last part of Gomulka's speech was devoted to the question of democratization. 'The road of democratization,' he said, 'is the only road leading to the construction of the best model of socialism in our conditions. From that road we shall not deviate, and we shall defend ourselves with all our might against any attempts to push us off it.' Was that last sentence also addressed to Khrushchev?

'We shall not allow anyone to use the process of democratization to undermine socialism,' said Gomulka, and this time the warning, directed to Poland, may also have been an assurance addressed to the Kremlin. 'Our Party is taking its place at the head of the process of democratization, and only our Party, acting in conjunction with the other parties of the National Front, can guide this process.' In other words, the question of a return to a full parliamentary democracy simply did not arise.

Speaking of the P Z P R itself Gomulka called for the appointment of a commission of inquiry, which would investigate the responsibility for past crimes and mistakes.

It is not a matter of presenting a bill for the wrongs I have suffered. Such an idea, as altogether any idea of settling personal accounts, is absolutely alien to me. These matters were too important to be changed into small and dirty personal coinage. . . . But the Party must consider its good reputation. The Party must be clean. And if anyone consciously has besmirched its good name he can have no place in its ranks.

Leninist standards must be applied in the Party, concerning the election of Party authorities, the open character of Party life, the right to maintain one's own views, while observing the principle that majority decisions are binding.

There must be, said Gomulka, a clear demarcation between the Party and the Government, so that everyone knew what he was responsible for. The Party should 'guide but not govern', and leave the administration of the country to the proper authorities.

Speaking of the role of the *Sejm* Gomulka foreshadowed a revision of the Constitution, which would restore the Supreme Chamber of State Control, responsible to Parliament. The *Sejm* should 'draw conclusions with regard to those persons who fail in the proper discharge of their duties'. In addition to the control of administration the *Sejm*, said Gomulka, echoing many recent demands, should truly become the supreme legislative body. The next election would be conducted on the basis of a new electoral law 'which allows people to elect and not merely to vote'.

In his final peroration Gomulka returned to the theme of truth:

What the present Plenum adopts will be carried by us, Comrades, to the Party, to the working class and to the nation with our head raised, for we shall be bringing truth. And truth, shown to the nation without disguise, will give us strength, will restore to the people's Government and to our Party the full confidence of the working masses. This confidence is indispensable for the implementation of our plans.

There followed a warning, which sounded like a postscript hurriedly added after the speech had been written. It was a warning to critics to be constructive, and an appeal to youth, which at that very moment was demonstrating in the streets of Polish cities.

We have the right to demand from our youth, especially from university students, that they should keep their ardour in the search of roads leading to the improvement of our present reality, within the framework of the decisions which will be adopted by the present Plenum. One can always forgive young people many things. But life forgives nothing, even youth's thoughtless acts. We can but rejoice at the ardour of our young comrades . . . we are, however, fully justified in demanding from them that they should couple their enthusiasm and ardour with the wisdom of the Party.

Having spoken for two hours, Gomulka sat down. It was now up to the Central Committee to accept or reject his programme of 'the Polish road to socialism'. Gomulka had made his meaning clear: there would be further democratization but no parliamentary democracy; more freedom of speech and thought, but no freedom to choose another political system; more independence from the Soviet Union, but no breaking away from the alliance with Russia; there would be fewer dogmas, fewer lies, there would be an attempt to obtain the consent and support of the population. Gomulka was offering Poland a more humane and a more pragmatic form of Communism, but Communism it still was—it had to be.

10

STORM OVER ROKOSSOVSKY

It was unavoidable that the VIII Plenum of the PZPR should be meeting in an atmosphere of tension. By the middle of October 1956 the Communist regime was shaken to its foundations; not only had the Party discovered that it had no support among the population, but the leadership of the Party did not even command the respect of its own members. Deeply divided, it was unable to undertake the long overdue reforms for which the nation was clamouring. Public opinion, having been mute for so long, was now asserting itself with vigour; it was demanding freedom, national independence and a better standard of living.

Everyone in Poland knew that sweeping changes had been planned and that within the leadership of the Party there was a powerful opposition to them. The vocal sections of the population, the intellectuals, the students and the workers, particularly those in Warsaw, were determined to prevent the reactionary and pro-Soviet elements in the leadership from putting a spanner in the works of what already they were calling their revolution.

The situation was highly inflammable. The dramatic and ill-timed visit to Warsaw of Khrushchev and three Soviet Deputy Premiers added to it a sizeable charge of high explosive, while the news of Soviet troop movements in Poland was threatening to act as a detonator. In the absence of any official announcement about the activities or intentions of the Russian forces, wild rumours were sweeping Warsaw about massive moves and counter-moves of Soviet and Polish army units, about the intervention of the Polish Security Corps and about bloody clashes with the Russians. The students and workers of the capital, who had been in the vanguard of the agitation for the return of Gomulka, came out into the streets, mobilized and watchful. They were ready to fight against any attempt at armed intervention and were demanding that the VIII Plenum should elect new leaders and get on with the reforms. In other Polish cities thousands of meetings were being held and delegations elected to carry to Warsaw messages of support for the progressives.

Behind the closed doors of the VIII Plenum some blunt speaking took place, blunt at least by the standards normally prevailing in the discussions of the Central Committee. All the speakers, with one exception, realized the need for circumspection when discussing matters related to the Soviet Union. They had to bear in mind not only the effect on the public, which was bound to learn sooner or later what had been said, but also the susceptibilities of the Soviet leaders, who would have every word reported to them. In spite of this caution, in spite of a certain amount of Communist 'double-talk', and in spite of some 'editing' to which the record may have been submitted, the following excerpts are from one of the frankest and most remarkable documents to be published in a Communist country.

On Saturday morning, when the Plenum reassembled at eleven o'clock, after Zawadzki's report on the discussions with the Soviet delegation, and before Gomulka's keynote speech, one of the members of the Central Committee rose to ask several questions about troop movements:

Starewicz: Comrades, yesterday, during those difficult and extremely serious conversations with the delegation of the CPSU, troop movements were taking place in our country in the direction of Warsaw. I don't know the details, for the army is not my concern, but from what I hear from comrades responsible for internal security there were several columns of tanks on the move towards Warsaw, there were some movements of Soviet units on our western frontier and inside our country in the region of Wroclaw (Breslau). In this connection I would like to ask Comrade Marshal Rokossovsky what was the object of these moves and who took the decision? Was it an order of the Politbureau, the Government or the Ministry of Defence? Also, when the decision was taken, did anyone consider the political consequences of such movements which cause anxiety in Warsaw and which undoubtedly threaten to create a deep misunderstanding between the working class and our army; did anyone consider the international repercussions of such movements taking place during such talks?

Ochab: The Politbureau instructed, and the Minister of Defence raised no objection, that no military movements should take place, with the exception of one small unit for special purposes. At the same time we were told that it is normal for some movements to take place at this time of the year. The reports, which we too have received, about movements, or alleged movements, need verification. The question of military movements is not on our agenda, but could be added, should the Plenum so desire, though I don't see much purpose in it. Does the Plenum wish to place army movements on the agenda? The Politbureau is opposed to it.

Alster: . . . there are many points which need clarification. They should be gone into and a report prepared for the Politbureau.

Ochab: As I have said we have received a number of reports, some of them contradictory. They need checking by the Politbureau. In my view it would be pointless to start a discussion on a subject of capital importance which has been insufficiently verified. The Politbureau appeals that this matter should not be placed on the agenda, but our statement accepted that the question will be examined.

Wasilkowska: I move that the Politbureau should report to the Central Committee on the question of army movements, which is a subject of very widespread comment.

Ochab: I agree. The Politbureau will consider how to inform the members of the Central Committee.

Putrament: Comrades, I don't think that what you are saying is very logical. We have a Government, we have a Committee for

Internal Security, we have a Ministry of Defence and a Ministry for the Interior—it is their job to know what is happening in the country, especially in their particular spheres. Can there be movements of army units about which the Ministry of Defence is ignorant? We have here the men in charge and one of them can tell us what has happened to his formations and the other what movements have taken place. The Central Committee must be told.

Rokossovsky: Comrades, everyone knows that the life of the country is following its normal course. [The official record does not mention the hilarity which allegedly greeted these words and some of the following statements by Rokossovsky, but then it does not register any reactions from the meeting, except on one significant occasion.] . . . The army has not received any decision from the leadership that there should be no movements of units and even if such a decision were received it would take several days to implement it. Comrades are aware that this is the time when the army conducts tactical exercises. . . . In this connection we have to use areas outside the normal garrisons. . . . The Politbureau is aware of the concentration of some units for special purposes. This has been done in connection with the experience during the Poznan incidents. Regarding the Soviet forces I received an instruction from the Politbureau to clarify the matter, because there were signals that there had been some movements. Indeed Soviet forces were moving. They were conducting autumn manoeuvres in the area where the Soviet army group has its bases. They were moving in the direction of Lodz and Bydgoszcz. In this connection I asked Marshal Koniev, who was in command, that the eastward movement of the northern group should stop and the units return to their bases. That is all I know.

Marshal Rokossovsky ended by assuring the Plenum that 'the army would not take one single step without an order from the Government and from the Politbureau'. This little speech brought the debate to a close. It was clearly unwise to press the matter further and there were no objections when Ochab announced that the Politbureau would investigate the reports about troop movements and, in due course, inform the members of the Central Committee of its conclusions.

The Soviet military threat was pushed into the background, but it continued to influence subsequent discussions and the elections to the Politbureau. By that time the members of the Central Committee had before them a list of nine names proposed for election by the majority of the retiring Politbureau. Rokossovsky's name was not on that list, which was headed by Gomulka and did not include a single member of the Natolin group. Some supporters of the Natolin group protested against the omission of Rokossovsky, hinting quite openly that it would do no good to Polish-Soviet relations. The most outspoken intervention came from Boleslaw Ruminski, who, acting on the well tried principle that attack is the best form of defence, started with a strong sally against the Warsaw Committee of the Party and its secretary:

We are meeting at a time when the streets are the scene of attempts at organized and unorganized demonstrations, which cause chaos and confusion. We allow some members of the Party to conduct campaigns against other members, and they are not too choosey about their methods of attack. . . . We have created a situation, in which the whole of the people's power and our whole system are not only under fire—that would not be disastrous— but we are approaching a state of anarchy. And who is responsible? Are the Warsaw Committee and Comrade Staszewski responsible for it? Of course, it is Comrade Staszewski who has to bear the greatest share of responsibility.

Later in his speech Ruminski said:

I don't understand why Comrades Rokossovsky and Nowak are not proposed for the new Politbureau, while Comrade Zambrowski is nominated for re-election. After all Comrade Zambrowski represents the old political line, the old tradition and the old mistakes. Perhaps in recent times Comrade Zambrowski did not support the old line, at least not always, and he has changed. But this business has a bad smell, especially in the atmosphere of the present campaign of an anti-Soviet character.

There were one or two other interventions in the same vein, though less outspoken. When, the following day, it was

Ochab's turn to speak, the Central Committee heard quite a different interpretation of what was going on in Warsaw. The departing First Secretary threw an interesting light on the mood of the people and also on his own character, saying:

During the past few months we have, and especially I have, lived through so many bitter experiences that I thought it would not be possible for me to have to swallow yet another, even more bitter pill. But the last two days brought new developments of unprecedented bitterness. In conversation with our Soviet friends, for instance, I met completely unfounded and unheard of accusations; there has also been the other phenomenon, not unconnected with the background of these conversations, but which is a distinct problem—I mean the declarations by students and workers and the statements made by many people and the resolutions taken at many meetings in Poland, which want to defend the Central Committee against the army allegedly threatening it, or against the Soviet army. Who could have imagined that we should find ourselves in a situation in which members of the Party, men who ardently desire the victory of Communism, would face such a problem, would reach such desperate conclusions about an alleged threat from the army or from our friends?

One could, of course, look upon this from the abstract and formalistic point of view and reach the conclusion that it is a nationalistic and a backward phenomenon. But this is a very strange nationalism and backwardness. It is not represented by the bourgeoisie or the ideologists of the broken up classes, but these desperate conclusions about the need to defend the Central Committee from the Soviet army are being reached by men who undoubtedly want the victory of Communism and the deepening and strengthening of the Polish-Soviet friendship. It is men, who are deeply troubled in their conscience by what is happening, that reach those desperate conclusions and want to defend the Central Committee in connection with real or alleged movements of our own or Soviet forces.

There were accents of honesty mixed with despair in Ochab's words. He did not try to belittle the crisis, he did

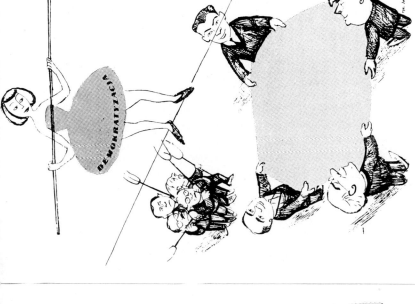

7. b. Tightrope act. Gomulka, Cyrankiewicz and two of their supporters are holding the tarpaulin; the Natolin group is waiting with pitchforks.

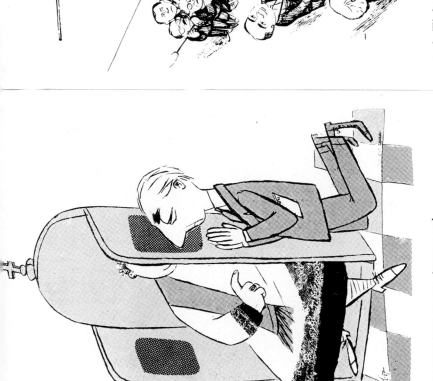

TWO CARTOONS FROM 'SZPILKI'
7. a. 'And you, my son, are you a believing Communist, or only a practising one?'

8. Gomulka casts his vote at the General Elections in Warsaw.

not try to attribute the blame where it did not belong. The students and the workers were not to blame he said; the leadership of the Party must bear the responsibility for the situation, and within the leadership his was the greatest share. They had failed in many ways and their mistakes produced the present crisis.

Ochab's interpretation did not please the Natolin group, which soon returned to the attack. This time its spokesman was Franciszek Jozwiak-Witold, a member of the Politbureau. He stressed the 'sacrifices' the Soviet Union had made on Poland's behalf and spoke of the 'furious anti-Soviet campaign' conducted by anti-Soviet elements. He said:

Some comrades have tried to explain that the roots of this campaign are to be found in some Polish-Soviet problems, which have not been settled and are causing dissatisfaction. . . . It is difficult to accept this theory, because the existing problems are not of the greatest importance and could have been settled within the framework of normal agreements.

Jozwiak-Witold appealed to the leadership and to the whole Party to

. . . act with the greatest firmness against all those who are slandering the Soviet Union and trying to stir up trouble between the two nations. I also appeal to the Central Committee to add the name of Comrade Rokossovsky to the list of candidates for the Politbureau. To leave Comrade Rokossovsky out of the Politbureau during the present stormy period would be politically unjustified and would not help the future Politbureau in its work. We must be guided in these matters by Party and political wisdom. These are important matters and they should not be treated recklessly.

The next speaker was Premier Cyrankiewicz, who gave a spirited defence of the workers of Warsaw:

Some see only hysteria and diversion in the present mood of the working class, and especially in the mood of the workers of

Warsaw. It is strange that the same comrades, who usually pay insufficient attention to individual and social psychology and thus vulgarize Marxism, should in the present situation resort to a psychiatric diagnosis instead of analysing the social background of the developments. And whose fault is it if there is hysteria and much impatience? Was everything that happened during the last few days conducive to calmness? We shall talk about it and draw the necessary conclusions after the present Plenum. There are some who see the hand of the enemy behind the present mood and are even beginning to formulate a theory about foreign agents. This is a worn out gramophone record. It has been played in our countries during the past years so often that it is scratched and makes a distorted noise. People who so desire can, of course, hold spiritualistic seances seeking inspiration from Beria, but they must do it in private. I don't deny the existence and the activities of our enemy, but in my view we must start by depriving that enemy of the springboard of our own mistakes, of discord, and of lack of leadership. If someone is afraid of malaria, he does not catch individual mosquitos but he drains the marshes where they breed.

Turning explicitly to Polish-Soviet relations, Cyrankiewicz asked:

Can one effectively fight the enemy on the sector of Polish-Soviet relations without removing everything that distorts these relations? Together with our Soviet comrades we must remove these distortions and this can be done only on the basis of mutual trust. It cannot be done otherwise. . . . Do the events of the last few days lead in that direction? No. We know it and we feel it deeply. We shall move in this direction in spite of all the difficulties, and this was also, in the end, the outcome of our talks, though they were conducted at a not particularly well chosen moment. The result of the talks opens this road, but the rest will, of course, depend on both Parties.

Cyrankiewicz associated himself with Gomulka's definition of the way in which relations between Communist countries must develop, and he added: 'Can anyone of you, comrades, indicate another way which in Poland would allow the leadership to enjoy full authority within the Party and the Party full authority within the nation? . . .'

When the Premier finished speaking, the Plenum proceeded to the elections of the Politbureau. Stanislaw Skrzeszewski proposed formally the name of Rokossovsky in addition to the nine names put forward by the leadership. Ruminski rose to second the motion, and made a last minute appeal for the election of Rokossovsky:

Ruminski: We are facing an unprecedented situation. We must admit that our deliberations are taking place in a tense and highly charged atmosphere. There is a tendency to increase that tension still further. . . . I am worried about the list of the Politbureau without Comrade Rokossovsky. My anxiety is not the result of emotion but is based on principles, on what is dictated by my Communist reason and heart. . . . I am afraid that we will not mend our relations with the CPSU and the Soviet Union, which are already strained, yes, our already strained relations, if we accept the list without Comrade Rokossovsky. This is a fundamental matter. What are the arguments against Comrade Rokossovsky? We don't speak about it frankly from the rostrum, but as becomes Communists, we should say openly what we feel and think. I have heard many good things about Comrade Rokossovsky, and during the last few days also some bad things, that not all is in order, that Comrade Rokossovsky's work is not perfect, that the conditions in the army should be different. That is one side of the picture, and not the most important side. What is most important is the interpretation the masses will put on the omission of Comrade Rokossovsky. In the present atmosphere the masses will understand it as an anti-Soviet gesture. Nobody spoke frankly about it from the rostrum, but in the lobby comrades have been saying that this is a way of exercising pressure on the Soviet Union.

Albrecht and Starewicz: Who? Who?

Ruminski: I am worried by this, but since you are attacking me, Comrade Starewicz, I will tell you—it was you. We were talking, I think it was the day after the VII Plenum. You said that Poland could not be independent, because Soviet comrades would not allow it and they interfered in everything. You also told me that

Comrade Khrushchev raised during the VI Plenum the matter of Comrade Zambrowski and the Jewish problem. . . . Comrade Starewicz, don't provoke me by asking who said it, because these are your views. One has to be honest. Comrade Wieslaw[1] must also have a clear idea who's who in the Central Committee, what they think and which way they are going.

The method of pressure against friends is not used anywhere. There is no precedent for using pressure on friends. [Here the official record reports 'commotion in the hall'.] Comrades, this method may, of course, sometimes produce results, but not always. A great risk is involved and I say: this is not the way, this is not the Polish way to Socialism. . . .

Ruminski's speech put the Plenum in a quandary. They did not want Rokossovsky in the Politbureau first and foremost because he was the symbol of Poland's satellite status, but none dared to say so openly. Now Ruminski was implying that if they did not elect the Marshal they would be putting pressure on the Soviet Union, and this was largely true. Any denial would sound pretty hollow and would be highly unpopular with the nation which demanded a visible sign of return to independence, yet an admission of exercising pressure on the Kremlin was unthinkable, especially with Soviet troops poised for action. The best course was to say little and get on with the voting. However, Starewicz demanded to be allowed to make a personal statement and the discussion lasted for a few more minutes:

Starewicz: In connection with what Comrade Ruminski has said about our conversation after the VII Plenum I feel obliged to make a short declaration, which will throw some light on Comrade Ruminski's methods. . . . It is true that we discussed the not quite normal relations between us and our Soviet comrades, but Comrade Ruminski was in complete agreement with me and in the end said: one can talk sense with you, one can agree with you.

Jaworska: . . . we have agreed during our discussion that one of the main reasons of the present chaos in the Party was the lack of

[1] Gomulka's wartime pseudonym.

unanimity within the leadership. . . . If the Politbureau now proposes a list of names, which we have in front of us, it is clearly of the opinion that the suggested composition will enable the Politbureau to lead the Party with unanimity and cohesion.

Ochab: . . . I would like just to point out briefly that failure to nominate someone does not by any means indicate a lack of confidence in the comrade concerned. . . . Comrade Rokossovsky's case is simply one of the many personal matters.

After this unconvincing attempt to remove the political sting from Rokossovsky's omission from the Politbureau, the Central Committee was about to proceed to the election by secret ballot. At the last moment Ruminski, who was clearly determined to play the *enfant terrible* of the Plenum and tried to make as much mischief as possible, moved that Gomulka's election should be by a show of hands, 'because members wanted specially to demonstrate their attitude to the changes which were taking place'. This was opposed by Gomulka, who insisted that he should be treated in the same way as any other member of the Central Committee. If it was Ruminski's intention, said Gomulka, to express his support by his motion, then it would be better 'if the support were shown not by voting but by carrying out the decisions of the Plenum'.

A secret ballot took place for the nine seats on the Politbureau. All the seventy-five members present cast their votes and all the ballot papers were declared valid. Only Ochab received all the seventy-five votes; Gomulka and his friend Loga-Sowinski polled seventy-four votes each (were they in fact opposed by one member or were they too modest to vote for themselves?). Seventy-three votes were cast for Cyrankiewicz, seventy-two each for Jedrychowski and Rapacki, while Zawadzki received only sixty-eight votes. Morawski, who had played a prominent part in the movement for democratization, and Zambrowski, who was the only Jewish candidate for the Politbureau, received fifty-six votes each. At the bottom of the poll came Rokossovsky with twenty-three votes.

The election of the members of the Party secretariat followed the same pattern, but there was no similar distraction to that provided by Rokossovsky's candidature for the Politbureau. All the seven candidates were elected and the new secretariat consisted of Gomulka and six of his supporters: Ochab, Albrecht, Gierek, Jarosinski, Matwin and Zambrowski. Then, by an open and unanimous vote, Gomulka was elected to the office of First Secretary; he had won the battle for leadership.

Rokossovsky was out of the Politbureau; the storm about his election was over, but it was not the end of the Rokossovsky story. Nor was it the end of the Natolin group; eliminated from the top leadership of the Party, it still remained an important minority in the Central Committee, as was demonstrated by the twenty-three votes cast for Rokossovsky. Given support from Moscow, the Natolin group was still capable of causing a great deal of trouble and presenting Gomulka with a serious problem.

11

COMMUNIST HEARTSEARCHING

IT is perhaps a legacy of the Stalinist era that Polish Communist leaders, even among themselves, cannot speak their minds openly. They have developed a language of their own, and the art of understatement among them has reached a pitch which puts British politicians to shame. When a Polish Communist speaks of 'distortions' of Polish-Soviet relations, he means gross violations of his country's independence, economic exploitation, etc.; when he mentions 'the cult of the individual', he is referring to one of the bloodiest terrors in history; 'violations of socialist legality' means mass arrests and executions of innocent people; 'lack of collectivity in the leadership' is synonymous with ruthless personal dictatorship. Also, Communism is usually described euphemistically as 'socialism', while the Russians are simply called 'friends'.

This curious jargon dominated the proceeding of the VIII Plenum. The Natolin group excelled in this 'double talk'; they were also using what one speaker described as 'a cypher language'—they were giving the impression of saying just the opposite of what they really meant.

At the Plenum there was general agreement that the Party was facing the gravest crisis in its post-war history, but when it came to the reasons for that crisis, the agreement ended abruptly. Ochab, in what was one of the most revealing speeches of the debate, gave a soul-searching analysis of the mistakes of the leadership. Polish Communists, he said, had been used to following the Soviet example and found it difficult to get rid of the habit.

I think that one of the reasons which created here the present crisis situation was the fact that we tried to apply Soviet methods to get out of what could be described as the post-Stalin crisis. I do not feel entitled, nor am I sufficiently acquainted with the facts, to judge how far the methods applied by the CPSU leadership are justifiable in the Soviet situation; probably they are justified. The Soviet leaders, taking account of their own situation, are defending themselves by very harsh methods against a spontaneous rejection of what is old, and are rejecting it in an organized manner, which can be evaluated in various ways, but which certainly does not meet our situation. We should have made the changes more boldly, consistently and speedily. . . .

This they had failed to do, said Ochab, and their failure was largely due to the lack of unity within the leadership. At the VII Plenum, after a discussion which was 'extremely heated and inflamed, during which everybody expounded his own arguments, without listening to the arguments of others', they were satisfied with a unanimous resolution, as if this could have solved the crisis. Instead of taking the lead in the process of democratization, the Party allowed it to develop spontaneously and the traditional methods of control produced no result.

Several speakers elaborated and developed Ochab's thesis. An ex-Socialist, Leon Wudzki, for instance, reminded the Plenum that it was not enough to adopt the correct resolutions. They had done so many times in the past, but they never succeeded in putting those resolutions into practice.

The theory was lovely, but in practice we had bureaucracy, laziness, opportunism, bigotry, jingoism, anti-Semitism and hypocrisy. In a way all this amounted to a form of indirect criticism of our system by the broad masses, who were not allowed to criticize us openly. The masses simply turned away from us, from the leadership. Why? Because we behaved like hypocrites. We said one thing and did another. We were impressed by power . . . we changed our meetings into solemn parades, into services at which we presented to the people various truths, in which they were to believe. Instead of teaching people to think we taught them to chant. In order to keep the nation in this condition, a nation which has a laudable tradition of fighting for freedom, we had to create an apparatus of oppression and resort to illegal methods.

Two of the men who, under Bierut, had exercised a powerful influence, during the Stalinist period were present at the Plenum, though no longer as members of the Politbureau. Both Berman and Minc made speeches in which they admitted many 'mistakes'. Berman pleaded guilty to a number of 'errors' but claimed that his sins were mainly those of omission and not of commission. He was guilty, he said, of having shown too much trust in the secret police, of exercising too little supervision over it, of copying Soviet methods, of not resisting some of the particularly flagrant abuses.

At the same time Berman claimed that he had learned of Gomulka's arrest only after the event (Swiatlo says that the arrest had been ordered by Bierut through Radkiewicz), that he was opposed to it and helped in preventing a trial based on false charges He also spoke of Soviet pressure to liquidate Gomulka and declared that thanks mainly to Bierut the 'worst and irrevocable mistakes' had been prevented. According to Berman he himself had been in danger, because Beria and Stalin accused him of spying and tried to involve him in the Budapest trial of the American citizen, Noel Field. Berman's secretary, Anna Duracz, had been arrested on false charges, and not only was he unable to help her, but he was himself threatened with prison and death from which he was saved by the persistent interventions of Bierut.

Berman's defence, though perhaps sincere, was not altogether convincing. The same can be said about Minc's speech at the Plenum. He also admitted mistakes—for instance, that the standard of living had been sacrificed for the sake of excessive investments—but he, too, blamed circumstances outside his control. The worsening of the international situation during the last years of Stalin's life and the consequent demands of the defence industry, combined with the Western embargo on certain exports, were, according to Minc, important factors in creating Poland's economic difficulties. All the same, Minc admitted that the root of the trouble was the system of government, and he himself could not avoid a share of the responsibility for it.

Again Ruminski proved the most outspoken and most provocative critic.

I have read Comrade Berman's self-criticism not less than three times. . . . Comrade Berman admits that he has acted badly, but immediately asserts that he has acted well. This we can't accept. In no circumstances can we accept what he says at the end, that he was in fact a victim of the system. . . . For everything that happened, so Comrade Berman is implying, the responsibility falls on our friends. This is no accident. A group of comrades is conducting a campaign in which they try to put forward the same argument also in the self-criticism of Comrade Minc. . . . They say and they write that Comrade Minc had been the author of the first, good version of the plan, but later a second version was imposed, which was not the work of Comrade Minc. Who imposed it? Our friends imposed it. I understand that Comrade Minc had to work in special circumstances. There was a special industry and much was being imposed, but Comrade Minc is also the author of the second version of the plan. Anyway, we know his policy. Were our friends also responsible for it?

The Natolin group was as emphatic as anyone else in the condemnation of the past and in its endorsement of the policy of democratization; they were also most adamant in rejecting anti-Semitism. To make their points they resorted to the 'cypher language' of appearing to say the opposite of what they meant. In dealing with the past they focused their criticism on the persons of Berman and Minc, who are both Jews, without mentioning their origin, which was known to everybody. They also expressed great suspicion of those people who had been associated with the old methods and now were claiming to be in favour of democratization, but they named only one of them, Zambrowski, who is also a Jew, while leaving alone the other converts to liberalization.

Zenon Nowak, one of the leaders of the Natolin group, protested against the anti-Semitic label which had been pinned on to him after the VII Plenum. Of course he was not an anti-Semite and everybody knew it, but he felt that the Party's 'personnel policy has often led towards anti-Semitism'. Nowak claimed that his only concern was to eliminate everything which may give rise to anti-Semitism.

Several other speakers also protested against the 'unjust and libellous accusations, which had been made against 'some comrades' after the VII Plenum. These were methods unworthy of Communists, which were weakening the Party; it was wrong, claimed the Natolin group, to give the impression that the Party was split into factions. Had they not voted unanimously for the resolutions of the VII Plenum? Were they not all in favour of democratization? Of course they were, but democratization must not mean licence and anarchy, which were leading to the destruction of the Party and to the weakening of the fraternal bonds of friendship with the Soviet Union. The furious anti-Russian campaign must stop, argued the spokesmen of the Natolin group, giving the impression that the Polish press was printing daily violent attacks on the Soviet Union; and those who, under the guise of democratization, are attacking socialism must also be given a strong rebuff.

In this way the Natolin speakers tried to confuse the issues. Only on one point—agricultural policy—did they dare to come into the open. Both Nowak and Jozwiak-Witold, the leaders of the group, expressed serious reservations regarding Gomulka's proposals to encourage independent farmers and to slow down the process of collectivization. 'We must realize,' said Nowak, 'that this amounts to a change of line in our agricultural policy,' and he was opposed to it. Jozwiak-

Witold was a little more discreet. In his view the proposed changes of policy towards the independent farmers needed much further thought, but he had no doubt that the slowing down of collectivization would be 'an unhealthy development'.

Unless one deciphered the language used by the Natolin group there appeared to be only the issue of agricultural policy which divided them from Gomulka and his supporters. Reading between the lines, and the Poles had become adept in it, it was clear that the Natolin group wanted not only to repress all direct and indirect criticism of the Soviet Union, but also to limit severely all freedom of speech and expression. It was also their intention to exploit anti-Semitism in order to gain popularity.

The Natolin group was not strong enough to force the issue. As the voting for Rokossovsky had shown, they could rely on the support of only about one-third of the members of the Central Committee. Gomulka's policy prevailed and the final resolution not only reflected faithfully his key-note speech, but also condemned the policies of the Natolin group.

'The Central Committee affirms that the decisive task on the road of Poland's development towards socialism is at the present moment the strengthening of the leading role of our Party. . . .' This opening sentence of the resolution made it clear that however far democratization may go, the Communist Party would maintain its privileged position, that there would be no democracy in the Western sense. However, the Party could maintain its position only if it were united and determined to put into practice the decisions of the VII Plenum, said the resolution, and it continued:

The Party must consistently overcome within its ranks conservatism and faint-heartedness, the fear of the new and the clinging to outworn doctrines and methods, the attempts to go back and to turn again to the old methods of leading and ruling, which suffer equally from Stalinist and native distortions.

Here was an open and definite rebuff to the reactionaries of the Natolin group. The elimination of those tendencies, claimed the resolution, was essential if confusion within the Party was to be avoided and 'the false liberal-bourgeois tendencies among wavering elements, particularly among the intelligentsia, were to be overcome'. It was also the only way of defeating those who were trying to abuse democratization by working against socialism and by trying to drive a wedge between Poland and the Soviet Union.

The Party was thus committed to a fight on two fronts against the Stalinist reactionaries and the 'revisionists'. But was the Party, weakened by internal strife and demoralized by the open hostility of the nation, strong enough to win on both fronts? The resolution foreshadowed a tough line against dissenters who were firmly entrenched within its own apparatus. 'The Party will not allow its decisions to be treated in a superficial and formalistic way, it will not tolerate comrades in responsible positions who avoid an active and consistent fulfilment of those decisions.' Here was a plain warning that lip service to the Party programme, in which the Natolin group had specialized, would not be enough in the future.

The resolution went on to describe the system of internal Party democracy which would be enforced in the future. All Party officials on all levels would be freely elected by secret ballot. Members would be given full information about the activities and decisions of the Party and their questions would be answered. Discussions of Party committees would not take place in secret.

The VIII Plenum also roundly condemned in its resolution some specific aspects of the Natolin policy. Declaring that Party members were entitled to their own opinions, provided that they abided by majority decisions, it added:

The Party condemns views and methods which introduce into its ranks artificial lines of division, according to national origin, it condemns all signs of discrimination against groups of people because of their origin, as this encourages anti-Semitism and all sorts of alien ideologies. . . . The Party's personnel policy must be based on principles and the decisive factors must be the political and professional qualifications of the comrades in question, their views and ideological maturity, their moral outlook, their ties with the working masses and their readiness to make sacrifices in the struggle for the cause of the working class. . . .

There followed a condemnation of all attempts to create a division between the workers and the intelligentsia, and this rounded off the first part of the resolution, clearly directed against the Natolin group and its policies.

The rest of the long resolution was devoted to a recapitulation of the main points of Gomulka's speech, and it concluded with an expression of hope that:

Polish-Soviet relations, based on equality and independence, will lead in the Polish nation to a feeling of friendship towards the Soviet Union so deep that no one will listen to any attempts to sow suspicion towards the USSR. The unity and co-operation of Socialist countries are the most permanent basis for our policy of strengthening independence and of peaceful development towards Socialism. . . .

This resolution was not adopted by the Plenum in its final form. The members of the Central Committee were asked to approve a draft and to empower its political and economic committees, acting together with the Politbureau, to work out the final text within three days. It was an unusual procedure dictated by the exceptional circumstances in which the Plenum was meeting. With the country in a turmoil, it was important not to prolong the session and to leave Gomulka free to deal with the crisis. On the evening of Sunday, October 21, the VIII Plenum came to an end after fewer than half of the members who wished to speak had done so. The remaining twenty-six who wanted to take part in the debate were asked to submit their speeches in writing for subsequent publication.

The VIII Plenum was over. Gomulka had won another inconclusive victory. He had stood up to Khrushchev and gained time, but Soviet forces ready for action were still on Polish soil. He had addressed the Central Committee and obtained their support, but there was still strong opposition within the Party. His next task was to face the nation and to rally it around him.

12

SPRING IN OCTOBER

WHEN Khrushchev and the other Soviet leaders descended suddenly on Warsaw and threatened to use the Red Army to prevent Gomulka's return to power with a programme of reform and independence, they were unwittingly strengthening his hand and turning him into a popular hero. They should have known that the Poles were not easily intimidated and they should have had at least an inkling of the true feelings of the Polish nation towards the Soviet Union.

Until the arrival of the Russians the internal situation in Poland was complicated and confused. The majority of the Party, led by Cyrankiewicz and Ochab, were pinning their hopes on Gomulka as the only Communist who had a chance of rallying around the Government at least a part of the nation and of restoring to the Party its self-respect. The Natolin group was plotting against Gomulka's return and wanted to control the situation by repressive measures. To a large section of the workers and students Gomulka was already a hero, but the broad masses of the population were more sceptical; to them Gomulka was another Communist, perhaps more honest and more patriotic than the rest, but still a Communist and the country had had enough of Communism. Seeing the Party divided and compromised, the majority of the people were hoping that they were about to witness the death of Communism in Poland and many were only too willing to lend a hand at the funeral.

The Russian intervention prevented that funeral in a way Khrushchev could not have intended. Having stood up to

Soviet threats, Gomulka became the hero of the whole nation and his chief supporters, Cyrankiewicz and Ochab, gained a new popularity, while the Kremlin's only allies, the Natolin group, appeared to the public as traitors. Suddenly the nation was united behind Gomulka, as it had not been united since the German invasion in 1939. But the nation was in an angry, defiant mood, ready to make sacrifices, ready to fight an unequal battle. This presented Gomulka with the problem of how to lead the nation without provoking the Russians, who still had their army poised for intervention. Gomulka and his associates faced this difficulty with great skill and courage.

The development of the situation during the days following Khrushchev's visit, the mounting wave of popular pressure and the various moves and counter-moves are best set out in strict chronological order.

Saturday, October 20

Khrushchev, Kaganovich, Mikoyan and Molotov left Warsaw early in the morning. The Central Committee met at 11 a.m. and heard Gomulka's key-note speech, which was later broadcast to the nation.

The news of the Soviet leaders' visit and reports about Russian troop movements caused deep anxiety throughout the country. Students and workers in Warsaw and other cities held meetings in support of Gomulka. Meanwhile some twenty delegations, elected the previous day by students and workers, called at the Central Committee headquarters to deliver messages and resolutions demanding a change of leadership and a policy of further democratization.

More delegations from Warsaw and provincial cities went to the Central Committee in the afternoon and were received by Gomulka, Cyrankiewicz, Ochab and Zawadzki. Gomulka told them that the new leadership of the Party would follow the policy of democratization, which had the support of the nation. Asked what were the guarantees that the mistakes of the past would not be repeated, he replied: 'You are the guarantee, the whole Polish nation, the working class are the guarantee of this.' Frantic applause greeted these words when the delegates on their return repeated them at meetings which were in almost permanent session.

At the Warsaw Polytechnic a meeting which began before 5 p.m. lasted late into the night. Thousands of students listened to speeches by the Secretary of the Warsaw Committee and the editor of *Po Prostu*, who reported on the progress of the VIII Plenum and Gomulka's interviews with the many delegations. Representatives of the workers from a number of large factories in the capital read out resolutions adopted at their works meetings. One of them received a special ovation:

We warmly support the composition of the new Politbureau and Secretariat proposed by the outgoing Politbureau and the protagonists of democratization. . . . We firmly protest against any pressure, from outside and by irresponsible comrades in the army, on the course of debates of the VIII Plenum. We protest against attempts to put the army against the nation.

At one stage the meeting threatened to break up in disorder when a group of youths started to shout anti-Soviet slogans, while others were calling for the release of Cardinal Wyszynski. A representative of the workers from Zeran climbed the platform, described the slogans as irresponsible and appealed to those present to keep to the point. The Communist majority complied and listened in a serious mood to the reading of extracts from Gomulka's speech.

The officers and other ranks of the Military Technical Academy in Warsaw also adopted a resolution supporting Gomulka and stressing the unity between the army and the nation.

The radio workers of Gdansk broadcast a resolution which firmly opposed all attempts at slowing down democratization. They also said:

We stand for inviolable alliance with the Soviet Union and the

People's Democracies, but we are of the opinion that for mutual benefit these relations must be based on the principle of a mutual honouring of full sovereignty. We firmly oppose all attempts at intervention in the affairs of our country, and that is why we demand that the real reasons for the visit of the CPSU delegation should be revealed.

The Moscow newspaper *Pravda* published an article by its Warsaw correspondent entitled 'Anti-Socialist voices in the columns of the Polish press'. In abusive terms the author attacked the Polish press in general and two Communist writers in particular.

At the VIII Plenum members of the Natolin group complained about the 'anti-Soviet' campaign in the country and about demonstrations by workers and students in Warsaw.

On the same day there were the first signs of a movement of Soviet forces in Hungary.

Sunday, October 21

The workers in Warsaw and some other cities reported to their factories, though it was a holiday. Ostensibly they wished to work in order 'to show their support for the changes which are taking place at the VIII Plenum', but the real purpose was to be at hand in case of trouble with the Polish or Soviet armies. There were meetings everywhere welcoming Gomulka's speech and protesting against the attitude of the Natolin group and its attacks on the Warsaw Committee of the Party. At a meeting in the Zeran works a speaker said:

It is difficult to foresee the final results of the discussions of the Central Committee. They depend to a great extent on our attitude. Our attitude in this matter must be clear: we shall not go along any road other than the one we have chosen and recognized as ours, the only right road; we shall not leave this road and shall not allow anybody to bar it.

A resolution sent to the Central Committee demanded the election of Gomulka as First Secretary.

Several Polish newspapers carried strongly worded replies to *Pravda's* attack of the previous day, pointing out that the article in the Moscow newspaper was neither true nor calculated to help Polish-Soviet friendship.

The Central Committee met at 8.30 in the morning to continue its debate and to choose a new Politbureau. The Natolin group pressed for the election of Rokossovsky.

Before the voting took place Warsaw radio broadcast an unscheduled commentary on Gomulka's speech. 'This is spring in October,' said the commentator, Henryk Holland, 'the spring of awakened hopes and of awakened national pride, the spring of true international proletarianism and of determined will to mark out our own Polish way to socialism.' Holland listed three essentials of 'the Polish spring in October': 'the great rehabilitation of truth', 'the rehabilitation of the true and the fall of the false authority', and the revival of proletarian internationalism which 'means equal rights for large and small nations'. The commentary ended with this passage:

> The spring is only in its beginning. The forces of the past have not yet capitulated, have not yet laid down their arms. Much vigilance, strong discipline, deliberation and great revolutionary courage is needed. But we have crossed the Rubicon and nothing can stop the great transformation . . . of the Polish Socialist revolution.

About nine o'clock in the evening the Central Committee elected the new Politbureau and Secretariat. The news of Gomulka's victory was immediately broadcast. Special editions of Warsaw newspapers appeared in the streets, where thousands were waiting for the outcome of the historic meeting. There can be no doubt about the genuine enthusiasm which greeted Gomulka's election and the defeat of the Natolin group, but the official announcement revealed nothing of the struggle which had taken place in the Central Committee; it did not even mention that Rokossovsky had been nominated for the Politbureau and had failed to get elected.

Excited by the hope of better times to come the people of Warsaw went to sleep late that night. In the provinces, too, the mood of revolution was abroad. The city of Stalinogrod announced that it was reverting to its old name of Katowice. In Gdansk a political mass meeting, which lasted late into the night, was attended by a Rear Admiral of the Polish Navy and, what is perhaps even more significant, by Wladyslaw Matwin, one of the Secretaries of the Central Committee, who must have left the Plenum before the elections so as to be present there. The meeting adopted a resolution demanding the resignation of the Secretaries to the Provincial Party Committee, because they had been 'hampering the process of democratization'. Three further demands were put forward in the resolution:

We demand the liquidation of the Office of Control of the Press, publications and entertainments. . . .

We demand the cessation of jamming of foreign broadcasting stations.

We demand that a new State loan be opened for subscription, so that we can pay off our debts to the Soviet Union.

Monday, October 22

That morning very little work was done in Poland. There were meetings everywhere, in factories, universities, schools and organizations, in naval and air force units, military academies and even in the General Staff. The jubiliation was tempered by sober thoughts about the difficult tasks ahead and the dangers still looming round the corner. A typical resolution adopted by the workers of a factory in Warsaw said:

The words of bitter truth about our economic situation and the conditions existing in the Party are better than the sweet lies which we have had so far. We clearly realize that our road today is difficult and will mean hardships and self-denial. Yet this does not put us off, for we see clearly before us a programme of action. The new leadership of the Party has been elected not only by the members of the Central Committee, but also by us. That is why we give it our full support.

Two of the Secretaries of the Central Committee spent the whole day receiving delegations which, according to official announcements, expressed a 'deep solicitude for the future of the country' and called for 'a consistent realization of the Leninist principle of equality of rights and sovereignty of nations'. It was pointed out at the same time that this would lead to a strengthening of Polish-Soviet friendship. Clearly the whole nation had been shaken by Khrushchev's visit and the still threatening danger of Soviet military intervention. Gomulka's difficult task was to keep them in check.

Monday also brought the first admissions that there had been an attempted military *coup d'état*. Curiously enough they all came from the coastal region, perhaps because the staff of the radio stations at Gdansk and Szczecin decided to ignore the censor in anticipation of the complete abolition of censorship, which had already been demanded in the previous day's resolution adopted in Gdansk. In the afternoon the Szczecin-Gdansk radio network reported several significant resolutions. 'We demand the full disclosure of the preparations for a military coup and the punishment of those responsible,' said the workers of the Gdansk power station. The Gdynia municipal Committee of the PZPR 'denounced all those who would wish to use the armed forces against the people', while from Szczecin came the demand that 'measures be taken against those responsible for the concentration of the army around Warsaw at the moment of . . . the VIII Plenum'. The harbour workers in Szczecin adopted a resolution asking 'that the Government speed up the repatriation of Poles from the USSR and the West . . .' and that 'the group of officers of the Polish army who during the VIII Plenum took up an anti-people's attitude be unmasked'.

In Wroclaw (Breslau) a torchlight procession organized by students to celebrate Gomulka's return to power ended in rioting. A crowd of youths entered the offices of the Polish-Soviet friendship society and partly demolished them. In the streets shop windows were damaged, Party slogans and also posters advertising a performance of the Jewish theatre were torn down, and groups of young people stopped passing vehicles, generally creating chaos. Similar incidents were also reported from the Silesian town of Gliwice.

Tuesday, October 23

The revolutionary atmosphere prevailed throughout the country. There were many more meetings, resolutions and delegations to the Central Committee.

Gomulka issued a message to workers and youth in which he summarized his programme, placing special emphasis on two points: the need to continue the policy of democratization and the principle of equality and independence in the relations between Poland and Russia. On this second point Gomulka repeated almost word for word the operative passage from his speech at the Plenum and added: 'This is how it should be and this is how it is going to be.' He appealed to the workers and youth to resist with determination 'all the temptations and suggestions calculated to weaken' Polish-Soviet friendship, assured them that everything possible was being done to remove 'the evil vestiges of the past' in the relations with the Soviet Union, and that 'positive results' had already been achieved.

One of those 'positive results' became apparent early in the afternoon when an official communiqué announced the dismissal of Rokossovsky's deputy, General Witaszewski, who had been regarded as one of the pillars of the Natolin group and its chief representative in the army. He was replaced by General Marjan Spychalski, a well known supporter and fellow prisoner of Gomulka during the Stalinist period.

Witaszewski was at the same time released from the post of Chief of Central Political Administration of the Polish armed forces and Spychalski succeeded him also in this key position.

It is interesting to note that the official announcement of these changes was worded with the greatest respect for protocol. It stated that the Politbureau had decided to direct Spychalski to work in the armed forces, and that 'in accordance with a proposal by the Minister of National Defence' (Rokossovsky) the Premier had recalled Witaszewski and appointed Spychalski in his place. This wording of the communiqué seemed to suggest that Rokossovsky would be allowed to remain the nominal head of the Ministry of National Defence, but Spychalski would be there to make sure of the loyalty of the armed forces.

Spychalski's appointment was welcomed in a number of resolutions by officers and soldiers, some of which were given nation-wide publicity by Warsaw radio. The Central Political Board of the armed forces also published a resolution pledging its support for the decisions of the VIII Plenum and promising to do its best 'to educate the soldiers in the spirit of boundless loyalty to the Party and to the Polish nation'. 'We are against all attempts to oppose the army to the people and the people to the army,' announced the resolution. 'We call on all generals, officers, NCOs and soldiers further to strengthen the brotherhood-in-arms with the Soviet army based on principles of equality and mutual respect.'

Another significant development on that Tuesday was a meeting between Gomulka and four Catholic deputies to the *Sejm*. According to a communiqué issued afterwards, the Catholic deputies assured Gomulka of their solidarity with the policy of the new leadership of the Party, expressed their readiness to mobilize the Catholic community to help in surmounting the difficulties, which were facing the nation and they 'brought to the attention of the First Secretary a number of important problems whose solution was awaited by Catholics'. This was the first official intimation of impending changes in the relations between the Party and the Catholic Church, a subject which Gomulka had left severely alone in his speech at the Plenum.

A further indication of probable changes affecting the Church were public attacks on Boleslaw Piasecki because of his article in *Slowo Powszechne*, in which, on the eve of the Plenum, he called in threatening tones for a limitation of public discussion. Catholic writers and leaders dissociated themselves from Piasecki's attitude and pointed out that 'he does not represent the whole of the Catholic movement'. The Warsaw branch of the Writers' Union held a stormy meeting at which Piasecki was attacked in even more outspoken terms.

Also on that day came the further admissions that there had been an attempt at a military *coup d'état*. During a stormy demonstration at Gdansk a militiaman (member of the civil police) made a speech in which he called for 'an immediate investigation of the foiled military putsch and for establishing the identity of those guilty', a demand which according to Gdansk radio was greeted with applause.... He also said: 'We demand an explanation from the Central Command of the Militia in Warsaw of its passive attitude during such an important moment as the VIII Plenum and the failure to inform us.'

A speaker representing secondary schools said at the same meeting: 'We do not want to go to school in Stalin Street' (stormy applause). 'We demand Polish textbooks written by Polish authors' (applause). He also called for the dissolution of the ZMP (the monopolistic Communist youth union) and the setting up of a new organization of all youth, without regard to their ideological attitude. He added that all the debts to the Soviet Union should be paid off as soon as possible.

The meeting ended with the singing of the National Anthem and the patriotic hymn Rota: 'We shall not cede the soil from which we sprang, we shall not allow our language to be buried. We are the Polish nation, the Polish people, the ancient tribe of Piast. We shall not suffer the enemy to oppress us, so help us God, so help us God.' This song, expressing the defiance of the nation during the period of the partitions before World War I, had not been heard in public for many years, but now, reflecting the mood of the people, it was sung at a meeting and broadcast by Gdansk and Szczecin radio.

An important mass meeting took place at Poznan and the chief speaker was Loga-Sowinski, one of the new members of the Politbureau. Addressing a huge audience, reported to number 'hundreds of thousands', he explained Gomulka's programme and said:

We are confident that the students, youth and workers of Poznan will prove themselves mature citizens and will understand that our independence can only be based on the power of socialism. . . . That is why we appeal to you for help. We appeal to you to show full understanding of and support for the new line of our Party. Your help may be urgently needed to prevent anything from standing in the way of the new line. . . .

The Poznan Executive of the PZPR passed a resolution in support of Gomulka's policy. It also announced that it was proposing to change the names of all streets and factories which had been named after Stalin or any living person. Similar resolutions were adopted in most other cities. Everywhere the supporters of Gomulka were taking over, while many of the pro-Natolin Party officials were either resigning or being dismissed from their posts.

Among the mass of messages and resolutions pouring into the headquarters of the Party, there were, however, none from Trade Unions or from peasants. The Trade Union Congress, headed by Klosiewicz, was in the hands of the

Natolin group and on Tuesday it found itself under public attack even from its own newspaper *Glos Pracy*.

Villages did not share the feverish atmosphere of the cities. Cracow radio reported that there was 'a lack of trust in the press communiqués' and that the prevailing atmosphere among the peasants was one of 'irresolution'. At the same time the leader of the Communist sponsored United Peasant Party, Stefan Ignar, was making a speech in the *Sejm*:

> In our country a national battle is in progress for the participation of the broadest masses in determining issues connected with our system, our independence, our sovereignty. The Polish people want to march along the path of people's democracy, along the path of building socialism.

While the Polish revolution was following its still uncertain course, outside Poland two events took place that Tuesday which had a profound effect on the 'spring in October'. In Budapest, what started as a demonstration of solidarity with the Poles, turned into the beginning of the Hungarian revolution and the first shots resounded in the streets of the Danubian capital.

In Moscow, the leaders of the CPSU reached a decision about the Polish revolution; Khrushchev telephoned Gomulka to tell him that the Russians agreed with the resolutions of the VIII Plenum and that Soviet forces would return to their bases.

We do not know if the last two events were connected with each other, but it is at least probable that the reprieve for the Poles was due to the blood bath the Russians were planning for Hungary.

Wednesday, October 24

In Budapest Soviet troops went into action. In Poland the tense, revolutionary atmosphere continued.

When the *Sejm* met in the morning to discuss the political situation, Premier Cyrankiewicz mounted the rostrum and made a brief speech. He referred to the policy outlined by Gomulka and the debates of the VIII Plenum and then delivered himself of the following, somewhat ambiguous, statement:

If anybody has any doubts as to whether anyone . . . during the debates of the Plenum transgressed the bounds of legality, I should like you to accept my statement that the Party and the Government, including the Minister of Defence, Comrade Rokossovsky—who strictly carries out the instructions of the Party and the Government, as is only natural—will draw the proper conclusions if investigation of these matters shows that anything of the sort did occur. . . .

The bulk of Cyrankiewicz's speech was devoted to Polish-Soviet relations. He argued that an alliance between the two countries, based on equality, was essential for 'the building of socialism in Poland and the Polish *raison d'état*'. Having developed this argument, the Premier made the following statement:

In reply to numerous questions put by the community on the subject of Soviet forces I can say, on the basis of an authoritative statement, that during the next two days all of them will return to their bases, the existence of which stems from international agreements of the Warsaw Pact. In the current international situation this Pact is still an important element of our security and that of other countries—of our security which, in view of German revisionism and the Polish *raison d'etat*, must not be forgotten for the sake of this or that sentiment.

In the evening an enormous crowd assembled outside the Palace of Culture in Warsaw to hear Gomulka speak in public for the first time in many years. He appeared on the balcony, surrounded by all the members of the new Politbureau, and gave his cheering audience a more popular version of his speech at the VIII Plenum. There were, however, important additions. Speaking of Polish-Soviet relations Gomulka said:

Our recent meeting with the delegation of the CPSU permitted the Soviet comrades to reach a better understanding of the political situation in Poland. [Applause.] Recently we have received from the First Secretary of the Central Committee of the CPSU, Comrade Khrushchev, an assurance that he sees no obstacle in the way of our mutual Party and State relations developing on the basis of the principles outlined by the VIII Plenum. [Applause.] All concrete matters affecting our internal affairs will be solved in accordance with the attitude of the Party and the Polish Government. It depends entirely on our view whether and for how long Soviet specialists are required in our army. [Applause.] At the same time we received from Comrade Khrushchev assurances that the Soviet troops in Polish territory will return to their bases within two days. [Applause.]

The next passage of Gomulka's speech, which was received in silence, dealt with the continuing need for the presence of the Soviet forces in Poland as long as 'there are Atlantic Pact bases in Western Germany, as long as a new Wehrmacht is being armed there and chauvinism and revisionism with regard to our frontier is being fomented there'. In view of this, said Gomulka, it was particularly important to 'rebuff any attempts at anti-Soviet agitation' in Poland.

Gomulka thanked the workers and students for their 'noble upsurge' in the last few days and 'the officers and soldiers of the Polish forces who have demonstrated their loyalty to the Party and Government'. He asked them to chase away the 'reactionary trouble-makers and various hooligans' who had come to the fore on the great wave of political consciousness.

The concluding passage of Gomulka's speech was an appeal to return to work and to show their support by increased effort. 'Today,' he said, 'we appeal to the working people of Warsaw and to the whole country: enough of demonstrations, enough of gatherings!'

The crowd acclaimed, they shouted Gomulka's name until they were hoarse, they sang 'Sto Lat'—may he live a hundred years. It was the moment of Gomulka's triumph, the victory

145

of the revolution. The Russians had given in, the danger was over, spring had really come in October.

But there were also other shouts in the crowd: 'Down with Rokossovsky!' called some, 'Rokossovsky go to Moscow!' shouted others, and there was the insistent chant: 'Katyn, Katyn, Katyn. . . .' For many thousands the victory was not yet complete. They wanted still more convincing evidence that Poland had regained her independence.

That night there were anti-Soviet demonstrations and riots in Warsaw and Wroclaw. A treacherous wind was blowing in spite of the arrival of spring.

PART III

ON THE TIGHTROPE

13

THE COMMUNIST AND
THE CARDINAL

WHEN Gomulka came to power he found that, if he wanted
to keep it, he had to walk on an endless tightrope, with grave
dangers threatening him and his country should he fall—a
prospect which would have dismayed a lesser man. A false
step in one direction could mean incurring the wrath of the
Kremlin and bringing upon Poland the onslaught of Soviet
military might; a false step in another could mean the loss of
popular support and an uprising on the Hungarian model.
What pleased the Russians angered the Poles and vice versa.

The Hungarian revolution made Gomulka's task in some
ways easier and in others incomparably more difficult. Soviet
preoccupation with the events in Budapest allowed him to
postpone his visit to Moscow, which he had undertaken to
pay 'in the immediate future' when he was playing the unwilling host to the uninvited Khrushchev and company; this
delay gave Gomulka time to consolidate his position at home
before he faced the Russians once more. At home, however,
the Soviet intervention in Hungary caused a great wave of
sympathy for the Hungarians mixed with indignation and
hatred of the Russians.

The people did not obey Gomulka's call to stop demonstrations. The anti-Soviet mood of the nation was threatening
to get out of control. Gomulka did not want to, and could
not take repressive measures; he had committed himself to
governing by consent and it would have been an ominous

beginning if he had to start by calling on the army and police to restore order, even if he could be sure that they would obey. He could rely on the workers and the students, who in Warsaw and other cities were organizing their own militia to fight local outbursts; this militia proved effective enough in dealing with the small demonstrations which followed Gomulka's public speech in Warsaw on October 24, but it would be quite inadequate in case of a real mass demonstration or rioting.

It was essential for Gomulka to gain from the nation more lasting support than the ephemeral wave of enthusiasm which greeted his appointment and his defiance of the Soviet threats. The demands of the people were: freedom, national independence and a decent standard of living. Gomulka's programme, announced at the VIII Plenum, fell short of meeting these demands. The freedom he was offering was limited to such liberties as were compatible with the continuing existence of the Communist system; the independence he was proclaiming was limited by the 'inviolable' and hated alliance with Russia. Only on the question of raising the standard of living did Gomulka's programme fully coincide with the popular demands, but precisely in this sphere, as he had warned the nation in his speeches, no immediate improvement was possible.

The Party was in a turmoil. Its apparatus had been largely in the hands of the Natolin group and Gomulka's election was followed by mass dismissals and resignations of executive committees and Party secretaries in the provinces. Even so the more impatient progressive elements were not satisfied with a spontaneous purge. The workers of the Paris Commune shipyard in Gdansk published an open letter on October 25 in which they claimed that 'despite the victory of the progressive forces in the Party leadership, supporters of the Natolin group remain in all sections of the Party and State administration. The Natolin group aims at restoring

Stalinist methods and at checking at all costs the process of democratization'.

In the villages the peasants were dissolving their collectives and dividing the land among themselves, without waiting for the necessary legislation. Party cells in many rural districts were disintegrating. In some cases the local Party bosses were taken to the border of their village, told to go away and not come back.

It must have been clear to Gomulka that it would take quite a long time before the Party could settle down and resume its role of an instrument of power. The situation, however, was too pressing and too dangerous to allow him to wait. In these circumstances, unable to give the people more bread, he decided to give them the maximum possible freedom and independence within the limits of Communism and the Russian alliance.

One step, above all, could prove to the nation that a new era had started, and gain Gomulka lasting public support— the ending of the ten-year war with the Catholic Church. This move did not figure in his programme announced at the VIII Plenum, perhaps because Gomulka did not want to alienate the Party diehards still further or possibly because he had not envisaged it at the time. In any case he did not hesitate for long; on October 28 Cardinal Stefan Wyszynski, the Primate of Poland, was released after more than three years' imprisonment. Early the following morning an official announcement brought the news to the nation:

As a result of a discussion between representatives of the Party and the Government . . . with Cardinal Stefan Wyszynski, the Primate Cardinal Wyszynski has returned to the capital and taken up his office. During the discussion it was decided, among other things, that it is desirable to set up in the near future a joint commission of representatives of the Government and the Episcopate, whose task it will be to examine matters requiring settlement in the field of the relations between the State and the Church.

These two carefully chosen, non-committal and not very informative sentences had a deep meaning for the twenty-five million Polish Catholics. They heralded the end of the persecution of the Church and brought proof that in Gomulka Poland had at long last a Communist leader, who was also a realist, who understood what the people wanted and put their wishes and the interest of the country above his Party's dogma.

By releasing the Cardinal, Gomulka was closing a grim and unhappy period in Poland's history. His predecessors, following blindly the Soviet example, had set out to fight religion and the Church. The struggle started soon after the war, but the grimmest phase did not take place until the last years of Stalin's life and immediately after his death. During that phase the Catholic Church was led by Primate Wyszynski, who succeeded Cardinal Hlond in 1949. He was only forty-seven, very young for this high office, but well prepared by his past work and steeled by the experience he had gained in his underground activities during the German occupation. 'I am neither a politician nor a diplomat,' he said in his inaugural sermon, 'I am your spiritual father, your shepherd, the bishop of your souls. . . .'

Wyszynski's aim was to keep the Church out of politics and he was prepared to concede all the demands of the State that did not clash with the canons of the Church. In 1950 an agreement was signed between the Government and the Episcopate setting out the principles of co-operation; the Church undertook not only to abstain from all political activity, but also to oppose the exploitation of 'religious sentiments aimed against the State' and to punish priests guilty of engaging in subversive activities. The Government, on its part, gave a number of specific guarantees, including the promise not to limit religious education any further and to allow the Catholic press the same rights as those enjoyed by other newspapers.

Jealous of the hold religion had on the millions of faithful, the Communists soon broke the agreement and did everything in their power to weaken the Church. They spent large sums financing a so-called 'progressive Catholic' movement, known as PAX, in the hope that it would help to undermine the influence of the Church. The leader of that movement was a very able and unscrupulous man, Boleslaw Piasecki, a former fascist now turned Communist stooge, who soon created not only a strong semi-political organization, but also a commercial empire, which enjoyed a monopoly of Catholic publications and of the manufacture and sale of devotional articles.

PAX was never more than a Communist front organization and was recognized as such by everyone in Poland. In spite of official support it never attracted more than a small fraction of Polish Catholics and clergy, but it was of some use abroad as the pretended spokesman of the Catholic community.

Side by side with the support of PAX went the development of terror against the Church. Hundreds of priests and several bishops were arrested, some of them tried on trumped up charges, others just held in prison without any pretence of legal proceedings. Cardinal Wyszynski protested in vain against this persecution and in the end, on September 25, 1953, he too was arrested and sent to a secret place of detention. The Pope excommunicated all those concerned in the Primate's arrest; from that moment there was an open war between the Communists and the Church.

After two years the Communist leaders realized that they had lost the struggle; the Cardinal's imprisonment turned him into a martyr in the eyes of the people and the only result of the persecution of the Church was an increased hatred of the regime by the broad masses. Suddenly the active persecution of the Church was suspended, but the Communists discovered for themselves that it was easier to start a war than to finish it; they offered the Cardinal a conditional release, but Wyszynski refused—if he were not allowed to return to his office, he would rather continue to live under illegal arrest.

It needed Gomulka, who had taken no part in the war with the Church, to make the decisive move. He was fortunate, and indeed Poland was fortunate, to find in the Primate a man who, though he was 'no politician and no diplomat', was however a statesman. And so a strange alliance began between a Communist and a Cardinal. Gomulka was no friend of the Church, but he recognized its influence and he knew how much he needed the support of every Pole. Wyszynski was no friend of Communism, but he recognized that in Gomulka the country had a leader who promised a more humane and more honest system of Government and the Cardinal too was aware of the nation's peril. Without any written or spoken agreement the two men, the Communist and the Cardinal, started to work for the common good of the people.

When the news of Wyszynski's release spread in Warsaw, vast crowds besieged the Primate's palace. Repeatedly he had to come out on the balcony to give his blessing to the multitude and to say a few words to them. 'Peace be with you', was his message and he appealed for restraint, order and a mature approach to the nation's problems.

The release of the Cardinal still left many problems to be settled before a proper *modus vivendi* between the State and the Church could be established. This was the task of a special commission composed of two bishops, one member of the Politbureau and one member of the Government. The Commission started work on November 3, but even before that date Gomulka made another step towards the reconciliation with the Church: he ordered that five bishops be released from prison. Wyszynski, too, did not wait for a formal agreement. The second Soviet military intervention in Hungary was threatening to envelop also Poland in flames; the nation needed wise guidance. On Sunday, November 5, Cardinal Wyszynski preached his first sermon in more than three years. Thousands of people filled the Church of the Holy Cross in Warsaw, and many more stood outside and listened to his words relayed by loudspeakers. His last, defiant sermon, just before his arrest, had been suppressed by the censor; now what he said was printed in newspapers and broadcast on the radio. His theme was suffering and love.[1] The cardinal said:

The twentieth century had brought terrible stains on humanity, and the human soul was crying out for the right of man to truth, the right to freedom, the right to some kind of justice, the right to love. . . . Modern man is ready to suffer and endure every deprivation and torment if he can only feel that these, his sacred rights, are respected. And this hunger of men, once experienced, will surely force a revision of many . . . contemporary arrangements, in order that men may be accorded in full the right to truth, the right to freedom, the right to justice and, even more, the right to love. . . .

The Primate stressed that further changes were needed in Poland to restore the fundamental rights of the people, but at the same time he sounded a note of caution:

We are in a period of unparalleled difficulty in our national existence, in which, at least for some time, we must speak less of our rights and more of our duties. . . . We must conquer the personal individualism that is so characteristic of our nation—and group individualism—in the strength of that love which we, always ready for sacrifice, must revive in ourselves for our country.

Poles, said the Cardinal, knew how to die splendidly, but they had to learn how to work splendidly.

A man dies once and is quickly covered with glory, but he lives in difficulty, in hardship, pain and suffering for long years, and

[1] A full summary and a translation of the main passages of the sermon appeared in *The Tablet* (London, November 17, 1956).

that is a greater heroism; and just that greater heroism is called for in these times, on this day so pregnant with events and so full of anxiety on all sides.

The Cardinal had spoken and millions of Polish Catholics obeyed his warning. In the hour of the nation's danger Gomulka had the support of the oldest and the strongest spiritual power in the land. He now proceeded to normalize the relations between the Church and the State. The various restrictions and repressive measures were eliminated one by one. At the same time, deprived of official support, PAX began to disintegrate.

A number of prominent people, who for one reason or another, had joined PAX, were now leaving it and Piasecki's organization came under strong fire from the progressive wing of the PZPR. Leopold Kurmand in the weekly *Swiat* (November 18, 1956) wrote:

In four years the political apparatus built by Piasecki assumed such importance in the overall picture of Polish Stalinism that there could be no question of a simple reward of merit; it was a question of an all embracing alliance. . . . The construction of entire new political formations rested on PAX. PAX emissaries went abroad. Their purpose was to usurp the representation of all Polish Catholics in the European forum and to mislead the public about the religious situation in Poland. When the talks [with PAX] in the offices of the directors of the Ministry of Public Security could no longer continue they were moved to the apartments of high dignitaries willing to take part in this type of negotiation. . . .

This was an open accusation of Piasecki as an agent of the old secret police and as a participant in the plot of the Natolin group. Discredited and despised, the PAX movement lost all its influence but, curiously enough, lingered on, and Piasecki remained at its head, waiting for a suitable moment to try to stage a comeback.

As PAX was fading, there were the first signs of an organized lay movement, representing the millions of Catholics. A Club of Catholic Intelligentsia was formed by a prominent writer, Jerzy Zawieyski; Catholic public meetings and discussions began to take place; a genuine Catholic press made its reappearance. The formation of a Catholic Party, however, remained out of the question.

By the beginning of December the joint commission of the Government and the Episcopate had reached agreement on all the main points. A communiqué issued on December 8 announced the new terms of co-existence, which largely amounted to a victory for the Church. According to the agreement new legislation was to guarantee the State an 'influence' on the appointment of bishops and other clergy, 'preserving at the same time the requirements of Church jurisdiction'. Religious instruction in schools was to be re-introduced on a voluntary basis and chaplains admitted to hospitals and prisons.

. The Government also agreed to the return of priests and nuns who had been expelled from the Western Territories and concurred with the appointment by the Holy See of five resident bishops in those territories, dropping tacitly the demand for the appointment of bishops ordinary, which the Pope had refused until a peace treaty confirmed Poland's sovereignty over the formerly German dioceses.

The Government also announced its 'readiness to remove the obstacles that existed in the previous period to the realization of the principle of full freedom for religious life'. In return the Episcopate declared:

As a result of transformations in public life, aimed at the consolidation of legality, justice, peaceful co-existence, the raising of social morality and the righting of wrongs, the Government and the State authorities would find in the Church hierarchy and clergy full understanding for those aims.

The declaration added that the Episcopate expressed full support for the work of the Government 'aiming at the strengthening and the development of People's Poland, at concentrating the efforts of all citizens in harmonious work for the good of the country. . . .'

Thus, under Gomulka's leadership, Poland became the first Communist country to practice religious freedom, while under the leadership of Cardinal Wyszynski, the Catholic Church, without surrendering what it considers as essential, declared its support for the new Polish experiment.

14

ROKOSSOVSKY GOES HOME

THE shouts 'Down with Rokossovsky!' 'Rokossovsky to Moscow!' 'Katyn, Katyn, Katyn . . .' which followed Gomulka's open air speech on October 24, the continuing anti-Soviet demonstrations and occasional rioting convinced Gomulka that his declaration of independence from Moscow and the removal of Marshal Rokossovsky from the Polit-bureau were not enough to satisfy the public. While he sought the support of the Church and released the Primate from imprisonment, he turned the whole of the propaganda machine on to explaining to the nation the need for continuing the alliance with the Soviet Union.

No responsible person in Poland advocated the termination of the alliance, but the masses, in their inflamed state of mind, were not capable of cool reasoning. The people saw the world around them in turmoil, with fighting in Hungary and in Egypt, they expected a war to break out any moment, and they did not want to fight on Russia's side. If they understood the warning provided by developments in Hungary, it made them only more bitter and angry. 'The Hungarians are behaving like Poles, the Poles like Czechs, and the Czechs like swine', was a current saying in Warsaw in those days. The Poles have always felt a close affinity to the Hungarians and the tradition of friendship was strong; now the Hungarians were doing what the Poles wanted to do themselves, and they were doing it in a manner which reminded the Poles vividly of their own brave but hopeless uprisings of the nineteenth century. At the same time Gomulka with great cunning was making positive steps towards independence, somewhat in the manner the Poles had come to associate with the Czechs, while Czechoslovakia, bordering on the two countries engaged in the fight for freedom, remained silent, except for official condemnations of the Hungarian revolution.

All this made the Poles uneasy and angry, angry also with themselves because of their inability to bring effective help to Hungary, and violently hostile to the Russians. 'In Hungary,' they were saying, 'the Russians have shown their true face, and here we talk of the eternal friendship and alliance with them!'

To counter this mood Polish propaganda was reduced to pointing out the obvious: the incorporation of the western territories and the new frontier on the Oder and the Neisse had not been recognized either by the Federal Republic or by the Western Powers. Polish newspapers painted in vivid colours the spectre of a capitalistic Germany, armed to the teeth by the Americans, and breathing revenge; and the only safeguard against Germany was the alliance with the Soviet Union.

This was the crude argument of Polish propaganda, but there was also a more subtle one: the Polish *raison d'état*, a phrase which suddenly became very fashionable among journalists and politicians. The Polish *raison d'état*, it was said repeatedly, made the alliance with Russia imperative, and the people, used to reading between the lines, understood that it meant: Russia would not allow Poland to exist if the alliance was broken. The poet, Adam Wazyk, who had greeted the October revolution with joy, now remarked sadly apropos of Hungary: 'We used to be the conscience of history, but now our silence has become *raison d'état*.'[1]

Not that the Polish press remained silent about Hungary.

[1] Adam Wazyk, 'Qui tacent clamant', *Nowa Kultura* (Warsaw, November 25, 1956).

It reported faithfully the course of events, it dismissed the fascist and foreign agents' theory, it rebuked the Czechoslovak press and the Paris *Humanité* for giving a false interpretation of the revolution, but it said not one word in condemnation of the Soviet behaviour.

In this way, by explaining the need for the alliance with Russia, and by speaking the truth, but not the whole truth, about Hungary, Gomulka hoped to keep the people quiet, while he was preparing further changes. The first step was the consolidation of the Government. On October 25 Cyrankiewicz announced the demotion of Zenon Nowak from First Deputy Premier to Deputy Premier, and the dismissal of four other Deputy Premiers, two of whom, Jozwiak-Witold and Stanislaw Lapot, belonged to the Natolin group. This weakened, but did not remove, the Natolin group's influence in the Cabinet.

The following day General Spychalski, the new Deputy Minister of Defence, issued an appeal to the armed forces. It began with these words:

In the great days through which our country and Party are now living, the Polish People's army stands at the side of the people. Soldiers and sailors, NCOs, officers, generals and admirals, the Party, the working class and the entire community thank you for not failing in the trust they placed in you.

Spychalski then warned the armed forces that every day sets 'new and more difficult tasks' and appealed for discipline, order and a sense of responsibility.

The next development was a conference on October 27 between Gomulka, Cyrankiewicz and Zawadzki on the one hand and a number of senior officers on the other. General Spychalski was in the chair and Rokossovsky's name was not mentioned in the official announcement. Forty-eight hours later the nation was told that Rokossovsky had gone on leave. On the same day the PZPR issued an appeal to the Hungarians to stop fighting and to support the Nagy Government and its programme; describing this programme the Polish manifesto explicitly mentioned Nagy's demand for the withdrawal of Soviet troops from Hungary.

On October 31 the Deputy Chief of the Polish General Staff, the Commander of the Warsaw military district, and the C.-in-C. of the air force were dismissed and replaced by officers who had been victims of Stalinist purges.

All these moves passed almost unnoticed under the impact of the Hungarian and Suez crisis. There were more demonstrations, panic buying of food, and other signs of mounting tension. Sensing the danger, the Central Committee of the PZPR on November 2 issued an appeal to the nation:

Comrades, Citizens! The Polish nation follows with great emotion the course of the Hungarian events. From the bottom of our hearts we have always been on the side of the Hungarian workers and all those who fought together with them for socialist democratization, against the forces which wanted at any cost to maintain in Hungary the old system of government hated by the people.

The Central Committee described the course of events in Hungary and spoke of 'the tragic consequences' of the policy of the former Hungarian leadership, which, instead of complying with the will of the majority of the nation, had called in Soviet troops. Lately, said the appeal, reactionary elements had begun to gain the upper hand in Hungary, but the defence of the people's power can be achieved 'by the internal forces of the Hungarian people . . . and not by intervention from without'.

The appeal described the different course of events in Poland and stated that 'the unity, the calm and the composure shown by the Polish community' had enabled the country to shape its relations with the Soviet Union on the basis of 'sovereignty, equality of rights and friendship'. Next the Central Committee explained that the presence of Soviet troops in Poland resulted from international agreements and was a guarantee of the western frontier. 'Here and there,' continued the appeal, 'voices can be heard demanding the withdrawal of Soviet army units from Poland. The leadership of the Party is stressing with all the necessary emphasis that such demands in the present international situation are contrary to the most vital interests of our nation and the Polish *raison d'état*'. The appeal ended with a call to the nation to stop manifestations and meetings, to keep calm, to preserve a sense of responsibility and 'for the sake of the independence of the country' to rebuff all anti-Soviet provocations.

The press was at great pains to show that Poland had already regained her independence. Jerzy Putrament, a journalist close to the Politbureau, asserted in *Zycie Warszawy* (November 3, 1956) that the first result of recent developments had been 'the de-satellization of Poland'. 'Poland's example shows', he argued, 'that it is possible to belong to the socialist camp—and only a madman or a traitor to our nation would wish to remove Poland from this camp—without in the least being a satellite'. Putrament saw in the Polish experiment the possibility of proving to the world that the 'dictatorship of the proletariat need not necessarily be merely a dictatorship' but can be accompanied by full independence and allow freedom of thought. The success of this experiment, wrote Putrament, would enable Poland to 'become a link between the two halves of Europe'.

This was an attractive idea, but it probably went too far to be adopted as official policy. The following morning Russian troops went into action in Hungary for the second time and the Kadar regime was set up by the Kremlin. A few hours later, Gomulka was addressing a national conference of Party officials. He was frank with them: 'The leadership of the Party is putting foremost in political work the question of consolidating in the consciousness of the whole nation the importance of friendship between Poland and the Soviet Union.' He spoke with great emphasis and returned to this theme twice. He did not disguise the seriousness of the situation and said:

Every Pole who loves his country and feels responsible for the safety of his nation understands the significance of the present historic moment. But there are citizens and comrades so hot-headed as to be guided not by reason but only by feelings and reflexes. . . . For the good of our country and for the peace of our homes we shall not tolerate any disturbances or rabble-raising.

This was the voice of a leader of the nation, and not just a Party boss. Gomulka did not forget, however, that the Party had to be the main instrument of his power and most of his speech was devoted to internal PZPR matters. There was to be a thorough reorganization and democratization of the Party; old habits of mind had to be removed, but there was to be no witch hunting. The divisions among the leadership, which came to the surface during the VIII Plenum, were to be forgotten; the present leadership was united and the Party needed all its experienced members who understood the new spirit and were prepared to put it into practice. There must be no discrimination, declared Gomulka, against people because of their political past or racial origin.

The speech of the First Secretary also brought the announcement of one more move likely to gain popular acclaim: the powers of the security police would be further restricted and in future they would be limited to fighting espionage, terror and other hostile acts 'directed against the rule of the people and the interests of the State'. The security police would come under the Ministry of Interior; the Committee for Security Affairs, which in 1954 following the Soviet example replaced the dreaded Ministry of Public Security, would be abolished altogether.

The day after Gomulka's speech came the next move in the 'de-satellization' of Poland: the dismissal of thirty-two generals and other senior Soviet officers, who had occupied commanding posts in the Polish army. They were replaced by Polish officers, mostly those who had been dismissed from the armed forces during the Stalinist period. Among those reinstated were two pilots who had distinguished themselves during the Battle of Britain.

The dismissal of the Soviet officers was performed with all the politeness at the command of the Poles. 'Thirty-two merited officers are leaving our army,' said *Zolnierz Wolnosci*, the newspaper of the armed forces, announcing their recall. The following week, at a formal ceremony, the Chairman of the Council of State, Zawadzki, accompanied by many dignitaries, decorated the departing Russians for 'their services to Poland'. Gomulka was not present at the ceremony.

During the second week in November the Natolin group decided to show that though it had been defeated, it was still capable of causing mischief. Five days after Gomulka's appeal to the Party to forget past divisions, one of the leaders of the Natolin group, Klosiewicz, the chairman of the TUC, mounted the rostrum in the *Sejm* and addressed a question to the Premier:

In connection with the diversionary news, broadcast by foreign radio stations on the alleged preparation in Poland of a *coup d'état* during the debates of the VIII Plenum. . . . I should like to ask the Premier whether the Government does not deem it correct and indispensable in the interest of the public good to announce officially its attitude in this matter.

Klosiewicz's question was well calculated to embarrass the Government and Gomulka. If they confirmed the truth of the reports, which incidentally originated from the Gdansk and Szczecin radios and not from foreign stations, they would have to order an inquiry which might lead to untold complications involving not only the Natolin group but also the Russians. If, on the other hand, the Premier denied the reports, he would be denying something which many people knew to be true and at the same time giving the Natolin group an undeserved testimonial of good conduct. Gomulka and Cyrankiewicz did not fall into the trap. On the morning of November 13 the Politbureau announced that it considered Klosiewicz's question as irresponsible and harmful, especially at a time when it was trying to restore unity within the Party, and that the Politbureau would move at the next Plenum Klosiewicz's expulsion from the Central Committee. A few hours later Premier Cyrankiewicz spent a good ten minutes dealing with Klosiewicz's question in the *Sejm*, but skilfully avoided confirming or denying that there had been a plot.

At the same sitting Cyrankiewicz calmly announced further Government changes. Among others, he recommended that the *Sejm* should accept the resignation of Marshal Rokossovsky and appoint in his place General Spychalski as Minister of Defence. The 'de-satellization' of Poland was complete, at least as far as the Poles themselves could achieve it; Marshal Rokossovsky, who symbolized the Soviet domination of Poland, was going back to the Soviet Union for good.

The following day Gomulka, Cyrankiewicz and Zawadzki, accompanied by a number of officials, themselves boarded the train for Moscow; they were going to pay Khrushchev and his colleagues a return visit. Poland watched their journey with anxiety and hope.

The visit of the Polish leaders to Moscow lasted four days and resembled little the tense and hurried talks in Warsaw in October. Everything went according to the established protocol. On the second day, November 16, there was the usual reception at the Kremlin and Khrushchev made a long speech about Polish-Soviet friendship based on equality, about Hungary, Suez and the world at large. Gomulka replied briefly, confining himself to polite remarks about the Russians. The Poles, too, gave the usual reception at their Embassy on the last day of the visit. Khrushchev once more made a long and emotional speech, mentioning past mistakes and different roads to socialism, approving Gomulka's election, promising eternal support to Poland, explaining Soviet policy on Hungary and other world problems. Again, Gomulka's reply was brief, polite and to the point. He admitted that as the Polish delegation was leaving for Moscow, anxiety had invaded their minds 'whether the leaders of the CPSU and the Soviet State would fully and properly appreciate the changes which have occurred in our country'. He was glad to say that the anxiety had proved unfounded and the agreement reached between the two delegations confirmed that the Soviet Government had meant what it had said in its declaration of October 30 about the relations between socialist countries being based on the principles of equality and non-interference.

The contrast between the speeches of Gomulka and Khrushchev was explained by the joint communiqué, issued the following day. It spoke of the unity of views of both delegations on such matters as Suez, Chinese representation in the United Nations and disarmament, but on Hungary it said that 'the delegations had exchanged views' on this subject. There followed a paragraph expressing support for the 'revolutionary worker-peasant government' without mentioning Kadar, and without any reference to the 'counter-revolutionary conspiracy' about which Khrushchev had spoken at the Embassy reception. Clearly on this point Gomulka was not prepared to go the whole way with the Russians, probably because of the mood prevailing in Poland. Another paragraph in the communiqué said that the discussions between the two delegations 'showed convergence of views' on the problems of the international situation.

A great deal of tough arguing must have taken place behind the scenes, but on the whole the Poles achieved everything they could have hoped for. They obtained from the

Russians a specific endorsement of their new policy and a number of concessions of considerable importance.

The Soviet Union agreed to cancel Polish debts amounting to the equivalent of 500 million US dollars in compensation for Polish coal deliveries in the years 1946–53 for which Russia had paid at prices well below the world market level. This was the first official admission of the economic exploitation of the satellites by Russia. The Soviet Union also agreed to supply to Poland on credit 1,400,000 tons of grain during 1957, and to provide long term credits to the value of 700 million roubles for the purchase of goods in Russia.

These economic concessions indicated that the Soviet leaders not only had decided to tolerate Gomulka, but were prepared to support him and strengthen his position by providing badly needed economic aid.

Other concessions were also included in the agreement. 'Both sides would consult each other . . . concerning the stay of Soviet military units on Polish territory, their numbers and composition.' The two delegations agreed that:

> The temporary stationing of Soviet military units in Poland can in no way infringe the sovereignty of the Polish State and cannot lead to interference in the internal affairs of the Polish People's Republic. . . . Movements of Soviet military units beyond the places where they are stationed require the consent of the Government of the Polish People's Republic.

In other words, the Russians undertook that there would be no repetition of their attempted intervention in October.

The last major concessions obtained by the Poles was the promise by the Russians to facilitate the repatriation from the Soviet Union of the many thousands of Polish citizens who for various reasons had not been allowed to return home.

Gomulka and his colleagues could go back to Warsaw with the satisfaction of a job well done. The Polish nation certainly regarded the outcome of the Moscow talks as Gomulka's victory and gave him a hero's welcome. They greeted him with joy and relief; joy because he had done well for Poland, relief because they had been worried about his personal safety (had not eighteen leaders of the Polish underground movement gone to Moscow at Stalin's invitation in 1945 only to land in a Soviet prison on charges of treason?).

From the frontier to the capital at every station thousands thronged around Gomulka's train, mothers holding up their children so that the young could see the great man, and everybody cheering and singing. In Warsaw the large Central Station was filled by an enthusiastic crowd. Obviously moved by the welcome, Gomulka said just a few words. As always, these were carefully chosen, but their meaning was plain: 'Comrades and Citizens! The discrepancy between words and deeds, which frequently occurred in Polish-Soviet relations in the past, has now been liquidated.'

The crowd cheered wildly, it acclaimed him as it had never done before. Was this Gomulka's finest hour?

15

THERE SHALL BE TRUTH

THE denial of truth and the all enveloping mesh of falsehood were among the most detested features of Stalinism. Not
only the broad masses of the population, but even Communist intellectuals revolted against the policy of lies; from
Wazyk's *Poem for Adults* to Gomulka's speech at the VIII
Plenum there was the recurring demand for truth.

The jamming of Western broadcasts was in Polish eyes a
particularly odious phenomenon, for people saw in it an
attempt not only to prevent them from learning the truth,
but also to cut them off from the West, to sever the age-old
religious and cultural ties and thus force them to surrender
to Communist propaganda.

It was no accident that one of the first objectives attacked
by the angry crowds in Poznan during the Thursday riots
in June was the local jamming station; this happened at the
time when a lessening of jamming was already noticeable in
Warsaw. Even before the VIII Plenum, a committee of the
Sejm passed a resolution demanding the abolition of jamming,
and this demand was taken up in many resolutions that followed Gomulka's return to power. The new First Secretary
was fully aware of the dangers of trying to suppress truth
and he had spoken at the VIII Plenum some eloquent words
about it. His election was followed by a further relaxation of
censorship; news reporting in the Polish press and on the
radio improved beyond all recognition and Polish journalists
availed themselves avidly of the newly won measure of freedom to express their views. One Polish politician was even

driven to the melancholy remark that all over the world, side by side with the opposition press, there is also a pro-Government press, whereas in Poland the whole of the press is in opposition. Like all such sayings, this was an exaggeration and an over-simplification, but it contained more than a grain of truth. The press, feeling itself secure from the threats of the Natolin group, criticized with increased vigour everything it considered wrong or inefficient. There was no shortage of targets for attack.

Two subjects, however, had to remain above criticism: the alliance with Russia and the dominant position of the P.Z.P.R. Watchful censors concentrated on eliminating from the press and radio everything that could be interpreted as an infringement of these two taboos. Western radios, on the other hand, could not be placed under a similar restriction, and this may explain a certain delay in abolishing the jamming of foreign broadcasts.

On October 31 the Cracow radio station announced that the jamming of Western broadcasts from that city would stop immediately and added:

The workers of the central administration of the Cracow radio station express their solidarity with the public opinion of Cracow province, and have decided not to use their establishment for jamming foreign radio programmes. The workers of the Cracow station have appealed to other workers' groups in the country to follow this initiative.

This was a spontaneous action in one city. Although it was welcomed in other centres, nearly four weeks passed before the cessation of jamming throughout the country was officially announced from the capital. On November 24 Warsaw radio stated that the decision to stop jamming had been adopted 'recently' and commented: 'The principle has prevailed that foreign broadcasting stations ought to be answered by arguments and not by noise.' By abandoning jamming, said Warsaw radio, Poland would save some 70

171

million *Zlotys* a year (more than £6 million according to the official rate of exchange) and enough electric power to supply a town of several thousand inhabitants, an eloquent testimony to the size of the jamming operation. Two months later, on January 24, 1957, the Director General of the Ministry of Communications announced that fifty-two transmitters, which had been used for jamming, were being converted to communications work and eleven medium wave transmitters had been handed over for broadcasting purposes.

When taking the decision to abolish jamming Gomulka must have been guided by several considerations: first, jamming was incompatible with his proclaimed policy of truth; second, it was ineffective and never prevented the Poles from listening to Western stations; the third, and perhaps decisive consideration must have been the support Gomulka had obtained from Western stations for his attempts to keep the country calm. The last point was admitted in an article in the daily *Życie Warszawy* on November 24:

It must be stated . . . that the decision to give up jamming is partly connected with the recently more objective appraisal of the situation in Poland by, for instance, the BBC. It is clear that the situation in our country can best be assessed by our public opinion, by the Poles themselves, and by the Polish Government. Should a difference appear, as is to be expected, between the appraisal made by foreign propaganda centres not always friendly towards us, and the truth about life in Poland, then the best road to follow is to explain the truth and engage in open polemics.

This comment was not an isolated case of Polish propaganda implying that a change had taken place in Western broadcasts and acknowledging the part played by foreign radios during the October revolution. On November 6, for instance, when the country was deeply shocked and angered by the second Soviet attack on Hungary, Warsaw radio broadcast the following remarks:

Voices of warning can be heard from all sides. Nowadays they can also be heard from quarters from which they have come only rarely hitherto. We think, said the London B B C a day or so ago, that Poles should preserve complete calm. The opportunity won by Poland's determination and prudence should not be lost.

Five days later the weekly *Zycie Literackie* (November 11, 1956) printed an article, in which the following sentence occurred:

Perhaps a lot of people are amazed at the Polish broadcasts from London or even Free Europe, which are soberly judging the programme of our Government and Party and appealing for calmness and prudence.

These quotations show that even before the abolition of jamming very large numbers of people in Poland were listening to Western broadcasts. They also imply that the policy of these broadcasts had somehow changed during the Polish revolution, a conclusion which does not bear close examination. It was not the Western broadcasts that had changed, but the situation in Poland; Western broadcasts merely registered that change, they noticed that instead of a regime of terror there was an attempt at governing the country by consent, that instead of being a Soviet colony, Poland was regaining a large measure of independence, that instead of a war against the Church there was a policy of religious tolerance, and so on. The B B C in particular always reflects British public opinion, and on the changes in Poland British public opinion was undivided; all British newspapers agreed that it was a dramatic change for the better, a praiseworthy effort to humanize the regime and to introduce a large measure of freedom. At the same time the British press showed concern lest some provocation might bring upon Poland a Soviet blood bath on the Hungarian model. All this was quoted in the B B C broadcasts to Poland and, coming from a trusted source, it helped Gomulka to keep the situation under control.

The BBC was the first Western radio organization to start broadcasting to Poland; its transmissions began in September 1939, while the Voice of America started broadcasting in Polish during the later part of the war; Radio Free Europe is a relative newcomer and entered the field during the height of the Stalinist terror. All three radio organizations have their devoted public, and very many people listen to all three. At the height of jamming in 1954 an American journalist reported from Poland that according to a confidential inquiry, conducted recently by a responsible State authority, some 500,000 Poles regularly listen to foreign broadcasts, despite jamming by Polish transmitters, and many more listened at irregular intervals.[1] These figures, coming as they do from a Polish Government source, are almost certainly on the conservative side. Radio Free Europe, which is on the air in Polish for nearly eighteen hours every day, probably has the largest number of listeners, but the reputation for accuracy and objectivity built up by the BBC since the early days of the war, attracts the more serious and the more influential listeners.

This is illustrated by a saying current in Warsaw after the October revolution: 'The four pillars of Poland are Gomulka, Cardinal Wyszynski, the BBC and the Red Army.' The contribution made by each of these four pillars is clearly of a different order, but the inclusion of the BBC was, at least, significant. Later, when Gomulka was forced to endorse the Kadar regime in Hungary and the BBC, again reflecting British opinion, mildly deplored this move, Polish propaganda showed displeasure with London, but jamming was not resumed. Under Gomulka the Poles were allowed to hear the whole truth from London or New York.

Internally, too, freedom of speech and thought made tremendous strides. With the secret police not in evidence,

[1] F. Kuh, 'Report on Poland', *The New Statesman and Nation* (London, April 17, 1954).

people were no longer afraid to speak their minds. Foreign publications were allowed to enter Poland more freely than any other Communist country and many more Poles were allowed to travel abroad.

The Writers' Congress, which met in Warsaw from November 29 to December 2, became a demonstration in favour of truth and freedom. Among its resolutions were demands for the abolition of censorship and of the list of prohibited books and publications in libraries and reading rooms, and for the widening of relations with Polish writers abroad. The Congress declared itself firmly against 'socialist realism' and State interference in literature. A new Central Board was elected, with Antoni Słonimski as chairman—a significant choice, because Słonimski, one of the leading Polish poets, had never been identified with Stalinism. An ardent admirer of H. G. Wells and his ideas, Słonimski was more of a liberal minded socialist than a Communist; having spent the war in Britain he returned to Poland and enjoyed a period of official popularity, but later, because of his attachment to freedom of speech, he became the object of violent attacks by the Natolin group and its supporters. His election represented the writers' endorsement of an uncompromising attitude in the defence of freedom.

While the writers were formalizing their divorce from the 'beetroot and tractor literature' of socialist realism, Polish journalists were assembling in Warsaw for their congress. They too discussed seriously their position in the changing system; they demanded freer contacts with the foreign press, an improved flow of news and other relaxations. There was, however, one basic difference between the two congresses. The writers were showing a desire to return to their literary work, freed from all restrictions and interference. This implied, and some of them said it publicly, that they would leave current affairs and politics to the journalists, who were now in a position to do their own job properly. The journal-

175

ists, on the other hand, had to deal with the political situation on a day to day basis and this, in the eyes of the Party, imposed on them the need for special restraint.

One of the members of the Politbureau, Jerzy Morawski, himself a former editor, addressed the Congress of Journalists on December 1. He paid a handsome tribute to the press for the part it had played during the October days, but he also issued a new directive. Morawski said:

Criticism is indispensable in order that we should be able to draw conclusions for the future. But if the press does not undertake a broader exchange of views and a broader discussion than hitherto as to what is to be the Polish road to socialism in the various domains of life, we risk not meeting the needs of the community. What matters mainly is the participation of the press in the working out of a constructive programme. It is necessary to probe life, to analyse and generalize the experiences and efforts of the nation. The press is doing far too little in this domain.

The Party was worried by the sweeping wave of press criticism, and tried to influence the journalists towards a more constructive state of mind. It was not an easy task, for at the same time the Party, according to Morawski, 'would not in the least deprive the journalists of their own initiative and independence'.

Both the Writers' and the Journalists' Congresses met in the shadow of the Hungarian tragedy, and their debates were dominated by the events in Budapest. The only thing the writers and journalists could do, however, was to appeal for help for the victims of the fighting and to send messages of sympathy. 'From the first days of your tragedy,' said the Polish writers to their Hungarian colleagues, 'at one with the entire Polish nation, we have been with you in your struggle and in your suffering. What is happening in Hungary is deeply stirring the conscience of all Polish writers, who know the importance, and the price, of freedom.'

A few days after the Congress one of the writers' demands

was met and the official list of prohibited books and periodicals, which operated in libraries and reading rooms, was abolished on December 5.

Press censorship remained. The Government wanted to preserve this instrument of control, but to use it with discretion, apparently suppressing only those articles which could be considered as an anti-Soviet provocation or as a direct attack on the Party.

In other spheres of public life in Poland the policy of truth and honesty was also bearing fruit. One of the most remarkable transformations took place in the Trade Union movement, which under the leadership of Wiktor Klosiewicz, one of the pillars of the Natolin group, had been a particularly dishonest instrument of Stalinism. Instead of defending the interests of the workers it had become a means of their oppression, while pretending to represent the working class. Following the VIII Plenum came the day of reckoning. At a stormy session of the Central Council of Trade Unions (November 16–18) the old leadership was removed and its policy condemned in no uncertain terms.

The most important speech was made by one of the secretaries of the PZPR, Wladyslaw Matwin, who attacked Klosiewicz by name, and admitted the 'degeneration and perversion' which used to dominate Polish Trade Union activities. Speaking of the future Matwin said this:

We shall have external and internal conditions for building a new socialism in our own way. We still do not quite know what this new socialism will be like. We only know fairly well what it cannot be like, what it ought not to be like. This we know from our own experience. We must do a great deal of work together to design this model, to lay its foundations, to make it—as a comrade . . . said last week—into the kind of socialism one likes.

Here once more was the honest and pragmatic approach, first demonstrated by Gomulka in his speech to the VIII Plenum. The Party, divorced from dogma, was itself search-

ing and groping for truth, while the successive layers of falsehood, imposed upon Polish life during the Stalinist period
were being removed one by one. This process of dismantling
the structure of tyranny without being able to offer a clearly
defined alternative was not without its dangers, as was shown
during the electoral campaign which began in Poland towards the end of November. This campaign was the next
severe test for Gomulka and his new régime.

16

THE TEST OF POPULAR VOTE

On his return from Moscow in the middle of October Gomulka had to turn his attention to domestic matters; a general election was facing him in two months' time, with polling day on January 20, 1957. If this were an election on the well-established Communist pattern, there would have been nothing to worry about, but Gomulka had promised the nation that it would have the right not only to vote, but also to elect. A new electoral ordinance, which was passed by the *Sejm* on October 24, provided that the lists of candidates should contain up to two-thirds more names than there were parliamentary seats, thus offering the voter a choice of candidates. Even this innovation would have meant little if Poland had been a single party State and only the PZPR were allowed to nominate candidates, but there were two other political parties in existence, the ZSL (Peasant Party) and the SD (Democrats). In addition, the law provided that candidates could be nominated for parliament by a variety of organizations, and that there could be more than one list of candidates in each electoral district.

The ZSL and the SD recognized, of course, the leading position of the PZPR and supported its programme, as did all the organizations which were entitled to nominate candidates, and they all belonged to the Communist dominated Front of National Unity. This prevented the embarrassment of having more than one electoral list in each district, but on the single list there could be only a proportion of PZPR candidates, and if the voters did exercise their right to strike

179

off the names of the people they did not trust, the Party could suffer an electoral defeat.

Gomulka could, of course, resort to the old Stalinist methods of intimidation of the voters and falsification of the results, but this would have been an open denial of all he had stood for in the eyes of the people, it would have been a betrayal of the Spring in October. The elections had to be free and honest, and yet the PZPR had to win them, if the whole system of People's Poland was not to collapse. Whereas there was no doubt about Gomulka's popularity in the country, his Party was only basking in the reflected light of his personal authority. Would this be enough to win the election? Could Gomulka find enough men in the PZPR who were free from blame for past mistakes and enjoyed the confidence of the public? The answers to these questions were by no means certain.

A further complication for Gomulka resulted from the sorry state of his own Party. The PZPR claimed a membership of nearly one million and a half, but it was, to say the least, open to doubt how many of the members were really Communists, how many had been forced to join the Party and how many had joined for purely opportunist reasons.

The satirical weekly *Szpilki* neatly summed up the situation in a cartoon depicting a man at the confessional; the caption read: 'Are you a believing Communist, my son, or only a practising one?' Even the believing Communists were confused and divided; the more rigid Marxists felt that Gomulka's policy was going too far away from Communism and they tended to support the Natolin group, while the confirmed 'revisionists' wanted even more far reaching reforms.

Gomulka opened the electoral campaign with a long speech to a meeting of some three thousand 'activists' of the National Front. What he said at that meeting, and especially the way he said it, provided an illustration of the tightrope act, which he was forced to perform on the internal arena.

His speech was in sharp contrast with the quiet and reasonable yet firm tone of his previous pronouncements. Here he was speaking as a Party leader, pouring scorn and abuse on the opponents of Communism, but at the same time he was opening up further vistas of freedom.

With the success of his Moscow talks behind him, Gomulka turned vehemently against anti-Soviet manifestations in Poland and claimed that the Soviet Union, after the past 'abnormalities' had been removed, was showing towards Poland economic generosity, whereas the Western Powers were always trying to exact their pound of flesh. He dwelt on the danger of German territorial demands and said that the presence of Soviet forces in Poland was the only defence available.

Next, Gomulka made it clear that people who were expecting the reforms of the VIII Plenum to be followed by a return to 'bourgeois democracy' were deeply mistaken. 'A free, independent and sovereign Poland can only be a socialist Poland, a Polish People's Republic,' he declared. There would be no freedom for all parties, as that would mean freedom for bourgeois parties which would not work for the building of socialism. People who were in favour of freedom for all parties, said Gomulka with scorn, 'would perhaps suggest that we should change our geographical and political setting, that we should move to another part of the globe or to another planet'.

Having thus reassured the members of the Party that he did not propose to go too far, Gomulka hastened to reassure the non-Communists as well. The framework of socialist democracy, he said, was not unchangeable, and he was firmly convinced that the day would come when 'socialism will have no framework whatever which might restrict the free activities of every man'. Gomulka stressed that it was not the intention of the Party to 'erect barricades within the nation' and that—

... the Polish road to socialism is different from methods of building socialism in other countries; among other things, it provides for co-operation with non-socialist and non-Marxist political parties, which yet support socialism. Such co-operation is possible because what is most essential in the meaning of socialism—the recasting of social relations by the abolition of the oppression and exploitation of man by man—accords with the aspirations of these parties.

The PZPR, said Gomulka, would contest the elections within the framework of the Front of National Unity, together with the ZSL and the SD, presenting the voters with a single list of candidates. This was, in his view, not a negation of democracy and he reminded his listeners of the situation in pre-war Poland, when twenty-seven different parties and groups contested the parliamentary elections, but the Communists were not allowed to do so, the workers were suffering from unemployment, and the country was poor and weak. Poland, he said, gained no strength from the large number of parties tearing her asunder and the pre-war 'democracy was not the same for everybody'.

The PZPR, declared Gomulka, would put forward the best men as their parliamentary candidates, and he invited the nation to elect them.

The First Secretary was followed by the Chairman of the ZSL, Stefan Ignar, who said that after the VIII Plenum the non-Communist political parties had been restored to their proper role, and by Professor Kulczynski, the Chairman of the SD. Both of them stressed the important new role assigned to the Sejm by the decisions of the VIII Plenum. Among other speakers at the meeting was also a Catholic leader, Dr Jan Frankowski, who welcomed the release of Cardinal Wyszynski and the prospect of the normalization of the relations between Church and State. He announced that Catholics would be participating in the National Front.

Thus the electoral campaign began. The people realized

that for the first time in many years they were given a chance of influencing the composition of the *Sejm* and took a lively interest in the proceedings. At local meetings in factories, offices, rural communes and universities some sixty thousand candidates were put forward. These were then scrutinized by the district committees of the National Front and eventually 722 were nominated for the 459 seats. About half of them were members of the PZPR, a quarter belonged to the ZSL, some 10 per cent to the SD and there were about one hundred candidates who were not members of any party, among them a number of avowed Catholics.

During the electoral campaign Gomulka's position was further strengthened by the Church-State agreement of December 8 and by the Polish-Soviet agreement about the stationing of Russian troops in Poland, concluded ten days later, which gave Poland formal guarantees against interference by Soviet forces. Within the Party Gomulka was reinforced by the visit of the Chinese Premier Chou En-Lai and by the joint Polish-Chinese declaration of January 16, which endorsed the programme of the VIII Plenum.

In spite of these developments the leadership of the PZPR was seriously worried about the outcome of the election. Members of the Politbureau and Ministers were touring the country, addressing hundreds of meetings, and they noticed an atmosphere of hostility. The Polish electorate took its newly won freedom quite seriously and speakers from Warsaw and the local candidates were subjected to blunt questioning; the tenor of many questions was hostile to Communism, to Russia and to the PZPR. Some of the candidates were also refusing to toe the Party line and even attacked their fellow candidates, accusing them of Stalinism. At least two candidates were removed from the official list for this unsporting behaviour. Finally there were further isolated outbreaks of anti-Soviet demonstrations and rioting, the most serious of them in the city of Szczecin, where the Soviet consulate was attacked on December 10.

All this made Gomulka and his associates uneasy, lest the nation might demonstrate its attitude to Russia and Communism either by abstaining from the vote, or by crossing out the names of PZPR candidates. The country was divided into more than a hundred constituencies, each of them electing between three and seven deputies out of the five to eleven candidates on the National Front list. If the electors did not mark their ballot papers, they were voting for the candidates heading the list, but the new law gave them the right to cross out the names of people they did not want to send to parliament. If the majority of the electors exercised this right, and crossed out the names of PZPR candidates, the Party would find itself in a minority in the new *Sejm*. This would be a severe blow to Communism, even though all the other candidates were also declared supporters of Gomulka and his programme. Large scale abstentions would have been an equally disastrous demonstration against the Party. Some of the less responsible opponents of Communism were in fact conducting a whispering campaign, trying to induce people either to abstain or to delete the names of PZPR candidates from their ballot papers.

In this perilous situation Gomulka received support from a quarter which could not be suspected of Communist sympathies; the Catholic clergy, led by several bishops, appealed to the people to cast their votes on the candidates of the Front of National Unity. 'We must give our vote of confidence in Gomulka,' said one of the bishops. The Primate himself did not express in public any view on the elections, but it is most unlikely that his bishops and clergy would have supported the National Front without at least Cardinal Wyszynski's tacit approval. The Catholic Church must have come to the conclusion that Gomulka's national form of Communism was the best system Poland was allowed to have in 1957.

In spite of the support from the Church, tension and uncertainty were mounting as polling day approached. On the eve of the elections Gomulka went to the microphone to make a last minute appeal to the nation. This was not just an election of the deputies to the *Sejm*, he said.

The significance of these elections lies first of all in the fact that we shall be choosing for Poland a road. In a general vote we shall pronounce whether we accept the road which was outlined for our country in the October days by the VIII Plenum . . . or whether we reject this road.

All those in favour of that road which guarantees Poland's sovereignty and independence, security and integrity of frontiers, internal peace and a policy of peace abroad, economic development and better standards of living for the working people, socialist legality and freedom to propagate the truth, those who support these most important points of the programme put forward by the VIII Plenum . . . should on polling day, first of all, take part in the election; secondly, vote without crossing out and elect as deputies those candidates whose names are in the top places on the ballot paper; and thirdly, encourage those nearest to them . . . to follow this appeal.

Gomulka turned the elections into a plebiscite, a national referendum which was to give him a vote of confidence. In blunt words he pointed out the dangers of rejecting his programme: 'To cross out the candidates of our Party means to cross out the indepencence of our country, to cross out Poland from the map of European States.'

The Poles understood what Gomulka was saying: the Soviet Union would not allow any other kind of Poland. They understood and gave Gomulka his vote of confidence. It was a strange election, probably unique in any country. There was no terror, no cheating, and yet 94 per cent of the electorate went to the polls and more than 98 per cent of the votes cast went to the candidates of the Front of National Unity (nearly 60,000 votes were declared invalid). Only in one district did one of the candidates fail to receive more than the 50 per cent of valid votes necessary to ensure his election.

When the detailed results were announced, it became clear that the nation had given Gomulka his vote of confidence, demonstrating at the same time its distrust of the PZPR. This was shown by relatively minute, yet highly significant differences in the numbers of votes cast on the different candidates. Gomulka himself received 99·44 per cent of all the votes in his own constituency, Warsaw No. 3. The second largest number of votes went to a non-party architect, third was a non-party Catholic writer and the remaining three PZPR candidates received the smallest number of votes. In other constituencies non-party candidates, or those belonging to the ZSL, headed the poll, while Communists were lagging behind. In Premier Cyrankiewicz's constituency in Cracow, for instance, a non-party journalist polled 97·3 per cent, while Cyrankiewicz obtained only 96 per cent of all votes; in Katowice Ochab had to be satisfied with 96·7 per cent of votes, while two non-party candidates polled 97·7 per cent and 97·95 per cent.

In this way the electorate made a restrained and subtle use of its freedom of choice. Gomulka won the referendum, but his Party was put on probation. In the new *Sejm* the PZPR had only a small majority with 237 deputies, the United Peasant Party had 119, the Democratic Party 39 and non-party deputies numbered 63 (12 of them were described as Catholic leaders). Only a fraction of the new deputies had been members of the previous *Sejm*.

The election was the closing chapter of the October revolution. A free vote of the electorate had endorsed Gomulka's programme. It was now up to him and his Party to demonstrate that they were capable of fulfilling the promises they had made. They had already shown their mettle in establishing a large measure of independence from Moscow. Now they were facing two even harder tasks: the improvement of the economic situation of the country, for which they needed time, and the maintenance of a precarious balance between freedom and Communism, which was likely to become increasingly more difficult as time went on.

17

THE BALANCING ACT

'ADVERTISER willing to exchange practically unused sovereignty for superior geographic position. Offers to Gomulka.' This apocryphal advertisement was Warsaw's favourite political joke during the closing days of 1956. It illustrates well one of Poland's insoluble problems and provides a key to the understanding of an important aspect of Gomulka's revolution. Poland, surrounded by the Soviet Union and Russian satellites, could be crushed at will; she is also condemned to rely on Soviet support in the matter of her new frontier with Germany. One of the nightmares that must be haunting Polish leaders is the possibility of a Soviet-German deal at Poland's expense, a prospect which no Pole, whatever his political views, can contemplate with equanimity.

Poland is thus doomed to remain a prisoner of the Soviet Union as long as the present international situation continues. The question of breaking away from the Soviet bloc does not arise, not only because the Russians will not allow it, but also because the Poles cannot afford it. However, not all the trumps are in Soviet hands; the situation resembles the old Polish saying: 'A Cossack has caught a Tartar, but the Tartar is holding the Cossack by the neck.'

The geographic position which makes Poland the prisoner of Russia also puts her across the Soviet lines of communication with Germany. As long as Soviet troops stay in Germany it is important for Russia to avoid any major disturbance in Poland, and the Kremlin knows that if it tries to interfere too much in Polish affairs it will have a major war on its hands. This consideration probably made Khrushchev decide against an armed intervention in October 1956. The Poles have thus a certain, but very limited, freedom of action which does not include either leaving the Soviet camp or introducing parliamentary democracy in their country.

Within those limits Gomulka has gone as far as he could. He has removed all the symptoms of Poland's colonial status, he has established something like an ideological alliance with China, and he has negotiated with the United States for economic aid; to a large extent he has restored Poland's sovereignty, but there are limits which he must not exceed, lest the Russians conclude that Gomulka represents a greater danger than the risks involved in the military campaign which would be necessary to subdue Poland. To go to the limit, and yet never to exceed it, even under strong pressure of popular opinion at home, that is Gomulka's difficult task in foreign policy.

In domestic affairs, where he has introduced the most sweeping changes, his task is even more arduous. By Soviet edict, and also by his own choice, Gomulka is committed to maintain a Communist system in a country which is strongly anti-Communist; this is made still more difficult by his proclaimed policy of governing by popular consent—one of the main achievements of the October revolution. To reconcile these irreconcilables Gomulka has to perform an endless balancing act, at one moment satisfying popular demands at the expense of the Party, and immediately afterwards trying to strengthen the Party at the cost of his own popularity.

Two measures announced by Gomulka in October 1956 illustrate this point. His new agricultural policy, which encourages the private farmer and abandons any attempt at forced collectivization, gained him wide popularity and support in the countryside, but alienated the more orthodox Marxist elements within his Party. Out of the 10,000 collective farms nearly four-fifths dissolved themselves—a vivid testimony to the unpopularity of the old policy, but a bitter pill for an orthodox Communist to swallow. The ending of the persecution of the Catholic Church and the reintroduction of religious education in schools won Gomulka nationwide acclaim, but incurred the wrath of the Party stalwarts, even though attendance remained voluntary. Soon complaints could be heard from Communists that their children were being ostracized by their classmates for keeping away from religious lessons and the Party monthly *Nowe Drogi*, in March 1957, described the reintroduction of the teaching of religion as 'undoubtedly a step backward'.

From the Communist point of view developments among the Polish youth were another step backward. The Stalinist ZMP (Association of Polish Youth), which had been modelled on the Soviet *Komsomol*, decided to dissolve itself and left the field to a number of new organizations, which were set up spontaneously after the VIII Plenum. One of them described itself as 'Revolutionary', another as 'Democratic', a third as 'Rural', and the situation became somewhat chaotic. If the Communist Party was to preserve its special position, it could not allow those 'anarchistic' tendencies to continue; official guidance or orders soon led to the dissolution of some youth organizations and the merging of others. Polish youth which had been looking forward to more freedom than is possible under Communism has had to be disappointed.

Every revolution brings in its wake some disappointed hopes, and the Polish revolution was no exception. Within a few days it achieved so much, it moved so far from the Soviet system that people began to expect complete freedom, which this revolution could not give them.

With the secret police no longer in evidence, the Poles can and do speak their minds freely in private and, with some limitations, also in public. It is only natural that having gained so much, the people should be asking for more, for the removal of the two remaining restraints, which put the alliance with Russia and the leading position of the PZPR outside the bounds of permitted criticism. This Gomulka cannot allow; he is in the position of a circus performer who earns his livelihood by putting his head in the mouth of the Soviet lion and he cannot afford to prick the lion, lest the animal's jaws suddenly close on him.

A similar position of restraint and uneasy compromise has been imposed on other sectors of political life. The two parties allowed to co-exist with the Communists have shaken off their Stalinist past and have become a little more like genuine political organizations, but they must continue to recognize the leading position of the PZPR and follow its political line. If they do this without reservation, they cannot expect much popular support and are of little value as allies of the Communists, but if they showed too much independence and gained too much popularity, they could become a serious danger to the PZPR. Another insoluble dilemma.

The new position of the *Sejm* is also an uneasy compromise between parliamentary democracy and the dictatorship of the proletariat. The *Sejm* is encouraged to perform parliamentary functions without being allowed to exercise the essential privilege of parliaments, that of deciding the political, economic and social system of the country. These vital decisions are the prerogative of the PZPR, which also takes all other major decisions of policy. The *Sejm*, however, is expected to be a true legislative body and to exercise control over a Government which takes its orders from someone else; it is expected to criticize the Government in an effective manner, but it is not allowed to have an opposition party or group. Many Polish politicians are aware of the basic contradictions of this system, and some are groping for a solution.

Within the Communist Party itself, Gomulka is faced with the need to reconcile the irreconcilable. The Natolin group and the whole reactionary wing of the PZPR want a tough

Marxist, not to say Stalinist, policy, while the progressive wing, often described as the 'revisionists', calls for further reforms, for a further dilution of Marxism and even for a return to genuine parliamentary democracy. Gomulka, who is not in favour of purges, wants to keep both wings in the Party, but in the effort to preserve his balance, he has often to call to order one or the other, and not infrequently both.

Where does Gomulka himself stand from an ideological point of view? On more than one occasion he has broken with the Marxist dogma, but occasionally he still pays it lip service. There is no doubt that he considers himself as Communist, but his definition of the essential and immutable element of Communism—the abolition of the exploitation of man by man—is acceptable to all Social Democrats and to many people who have little sympathy with socialism. In his programme speech at the VIII Plenum, Gomulka also said that it was a poor idea that socialism could be built only by people professing a materialistic social ideology.

Perhaps the years spent in solitary confinement, where his Stalinist colleagues had put him, gave Gomulka a chance to re-think his ideology. This has led him to the abandonment of rigidity, to a pragmatic, almost experimental approach to the problems of Poland. It also gave him an appreciation of human values and the humility of a man who does not know and does not pretend to know all the answers.

Perhaps the best illustration is provided by Gomulka's economic policy. He has moved away from rigid central planning and in January 1957 he abolished the State Planning Commission. Decentralization became the policy in Poland several months before Khrushchev adopted it in the Soviet Union. Gomulka is also in favour of workers' participation in the management of industry somewhat on the Yugoslav pattern, but on this point he was very cautious in his speech at the VIII Plenum and recommended limited experiments. The impatient workers in many factories went ahead on their own and this spontaneous movement threatened to cause chaos, especially because in some establishments they threw out well qualified managers and tried to run things on their own. The Government had to call a halt, reinstate most of the managers and re-think the whole problem. The final pattern is not yet clear.

The position of the workers has improved considerably by the abolition of the harsh labour discipline; strikes are no longer punished, though, of course they are discouraged; the Trade Unions show more concern for the welfare of their members and less for Government directives; they are no longer just a 'transmission line' for orders from above. The standard of living of the workers remains, however, frighteningly low and is likely to remain so until the supply of food and consumer goods improve. This is Gomulka's most pressing problem and his whole economic policy is directed towards its solution. Heavy industry has lost its old priority and large investments are planned in the consumer industries, housing and agriculture, but no quick results can be expected. In the meantime Gomulka must rely on outside help to satisfy the pressing needs of the population. The Soviet supplies of grain and the credits he obtained during his visit to Moscow in November 1956 are not enough, hence Poland's desire for large-scale American aid.

When Gomulka came to power, he started with a fund of good will among the people; he told them bluntly that economic miracles did not happen and that only more production could bring them a higher standard of living; at the beginning the workers showed an understanding of the position, they have also enjoyed the other fruits of the revolution, but sooner or later they will start protesting loudly if their material conditions do not improve. For Gomulka it is a race against time.

If he succeeds in solving the economic crisis, he will still be left with the basic contradictions of his system, he will still

o   193

have to continue his balancing act between Communism and popularity, between the right and the left wings of his Party, between freedom and the dictatorship of the proletariat.

In spite of all the difficulties in Gomulka's path, the Polish example is viewed with envy by the less fortunate inhabitants of the remaining Soviet satellites. The following trivial story from Czechoslovakia illustrates this mood:

On the Polish-Czech border two dogs met; one is on the way from Warsaw to Prague and the other is making the same journey in the opposite direction. They engage in conversation.

Czech dog: Why are you going to Prague?

Polish dog: I want to buy some earrings for my wife. But why are you going to Warsaw? There's nothing in the shops.

Czech dog: I . . . I just want to bark.

The Polish example can prove contagious, and if it does, it may in the long run lead to a peaceful dissolution of the Soviet empire. Will the Russians allow it to succeed? And if they do, will Gomulka be able to solve his own problems?

The obstacles in his path to success are formidable. Here is a nation proud of its long history, reckless in character, violently anti-Russian, passionately idealistic, devoutly Catholic and strongly anti-Communist, which is forced to be an ally of the Soviet Union and compelled to have a Communist system; a highly explosive and dangerous state of affairs. The situation was, however, even more dangerous and explosive in the revolutionary atmosphere of October and November 1956, when the Hungarian tragedy was threatening to spread to Poland. In those days the leading elements of the nation showed wisdom, prudence and an acute appreciation of political realities, they showed all the qualities with which the Polish nation has seldom been credited in the past.

As Cardinal Wyszynski said in his sermon in November, the Poles have always known how to die bravely, but now they had to learn how to live bravely. Maybe they are learning this lesson. There are signs from Poland that the thinking people are groping for ways and means of modifying their present system, but they are not thinking of overthrowing it, for they are convinced that the only alternative at present is a return to the more brutal, more oppressive indirect or direct Soviet rule.

Perhaps the most frightening thing about Poland's present position is the country's dependence on one man. Without Gomulka October 1956 almost certainly would have brought bloodshed and tragedy. Can the Polish experiments survive should Gomulka not be there to lead it? There is no obvious successor who would enjoy the same support from the nation, but many men around Gomulka have grown in stature since the revolution, notably Cyrankiewicz and Ochab; there are also several promising younger men who have come to the fore. Would they be able to continue successfully Gomulka's dangerous tightrope act, and can Gomulka go on with it himself, without suddenly losing balance?

He and his country face heavy odds, but it is worth while remembering H. A. L. Fisher's dictum that the history of Poland has been a series of surprises; the October revolution of 1956 has already added a few to that series and there may be more to come.

GLOSSARY AND ABBREVIATIONS

cc   Central Committee.

cpsu   The Communist Party of the Soviet Union.

Council of State   A body elected by the *Sejm* and empowered to legislate by decree while the *Sejm* is not sitting. The Chairman of the Council of State acts as the titular Head of State.

First Secretary   The chief officer pf the ozpr and leader of the Party. He is assisted by six Secretaries of the pzpr.

Kulak   (From the Russian) A peasant who owns more than a small plot of land.

Plenum   Plenary session of the Central Committee of the pzpr.

Politbureau   The Political Bureau of the pzpr is the highest council of the Party.

ppr   Polish Workers' Party, the name of the Communist Party which was set up during World War II.

pps   Polish Socialist Party, which in 1948 was forced to merge with the ppr, forming the pzpr.

pzpr   Polish United Workers' Party, the Communist Party in Poland, formed by the merger of the ppr and the pps.

sd   The Democratic Party, allied to the Communists.

Sejm   Parliament.

zmp   The Communist Association of Polish Youth, which dissolved itself after the revolution of 1956.

zsl   The United Peasant Party, allied to the Communists.

CHRONOLOGY OF EVENTS

1954

Sept.–Oct.	Lt-Col Swiatlo's broadcasts to Poland.
Dec. 8	Ministry of Public Security abolished.
Dec. 24	Gomulka released.

1955

Jan. 21–24	III Plenum of the PZPR adopts the policy of 'democratization'.
Jan. 27	A purge of the secret police begins.
Aug. 21	Publication of the *Poem for Adults*.

1956

Feb. 19	Announcement of the rehabilitation of the pre-war Communist Party of Poland.
Feb. 25	Khrushchev's 'secret' speech about Stalin.
March 10	*Trybuna Ludu* criticizes Stalin.
March 12	Bierut dies in Moscow.
March 16–23	Khrushchev in Warsaw.
March 21	Edward Ochab elected First Secretary of PZPR.
April 6	Ochab speaks of 'hysteria' among some Party members, announces the release of Gomulka but condemns his ideology.
April 20	Draft amnesty Bill published. It came into force on April 27.
April 23	Further purge of secret police.
April 23–28	*Sejm* session; deputies criticize the Government and some vote against a Government bill.
April 29	Ochab, writing in the Moscow *Pravda*, warns the Polish press against anti-Soviet outbursts.
May 7	Jakob Berman 'resigns' from the Government and Politbureau.
June 4	Announcement of the release, under the amnesty, of 28,000 prisoners, including 1,300 sentenced for political crimes.
June 28–29	Rioting in Poznan.

June 29	Premier Cyrankiewicz admits that Poznan workers had legitimate grievances, but blames provocateurs for the riots.
July 18–28	VII Plenum of the PZPR.
July 21	Bulganin and Zhukov arrive in Warsaw. Bulganin accuses hostile agents of organizing the Poznan riots and calls for greater vigilance and the strengthening of the dictatorship of proletariat.
July 28	VII Plenum ends with announcement that 'democratization' is to continue. New five-year plan is to raise wages by 30 per cent. Artisans and small farmers to be encouraged.
Aug. 4	Official announcement of Gomulka's readmission to the PZPR.
Aug. 24	General Komar, a supporter of Gomulka, appointed to command the Internal Security Corps.
Aug. 26	One million pilgrims attend celebrations at the national Shrine of Czestochowa.
Sept. 5–12	The autumn session of the *Sejm*. Demands for an elected, responsible and controlled leadership.
Sept. 27	The first Poznan trial begins.
Oct. 8–12	Verdicts in the first two Poznan trials; some of the accused acquitted, others given lenient sentences.
Oct. 9	Resignation of Hilary Minc, First Deputy Premier in charge of economic affairs.
Oct. 16	Announcement that Gomulka and three of his supporters will attend the forthcoming Plenum.
Oct. 18	Plot to arrest Gomulka fails. Soviet troop movements in Poland and East Germany.
Oct. 19	VIII Plenum meets. Khrushchev, Kaganovich, Mikoyan and Molotov arrive unexpectedly in Warsaw.
Oct. 20	Departure of the Soviet leaders. Gomulka announces his programme of reform and national independence.
Oct. 21	Gomulka becomes First Secretary. All Stalinists lose seats in the Politbureau.
Oct. 23	General Marian Spychalski becomes Deputy Minister of Defence.

198

Oct. 24	New electoral law; the number of candidates to exceed the number of seats. General elections for the *Sejm* to be held on January 20, 1957.
Oct. 28	Release of Cardinal Wyszynski.
Nov. 5	Thirty-two Soviet officers leave the Polish armed forces.
Nov. 13	General Spychalski replaces Marshal Rokossovsky as Minister of Defence.
Nov. 14	Gomulka and Cyrankiewicz leave for Moscow.
Nov. 18	Polish-Soviet declaration issued in Moscow announces the cancellation of Polish 'debts', further Soviet loans to Poland. Soviet troops to stay in Poland 'for the time being'.
Nov. 24	Poland abolishes jamming of foreign broadcasts.
Nov. 29	Congress of Polish writers condemns socialist realism.
Dec. 8	Agreement between Church and State.
Dec. 17	Polish-Soviet agreement on the stationing of Soviet troops in Poland.

1957

Jan. 2	The State Planning Commission is abolished.
Jan. 6	The Economic Plan for 1957 introduces cuts in the investment in heavy and defence industries, while increasing investment in private farms and housing.
Jan. 11	Chou En Lai arrives in Warsaw.
Jan. 16	A Polish-Chinese declaration supports Gomulka's programme.
Jan. 19	Gomulka's last minute appeal to electors.
Jan. 20	General Election.

INDEX

Agriculture (*see also* Collectivization *and* Economic situation), 24, 37, 43, 60, 63, 100–1, 105–6, 127–8, 189, 193
Albrecht, Jerzy, secretary of the PZPR, 119, 122
Alster, member of CC, 113
American aid, 193
Amnesty, 39
Anti-Semitism, 60, 63, 120, 124, 126–7, 130, 139
Armed Forces, in exile, 4, 12; under Soviet control, 15; in Poznan riots, 51–2; reactionaries hope for their support, 87, 112–14, 116; support the progressives, 88, 96–7, 134; criticism of, 119; attempted military *coup d'état*, 138, 141, 144, 165; support decisions of VIII Plenum, 140, 145; changes in command, 162; Soviet officers dismissed, 165
Army, *see* Armed Forces
Arts, *see* Socialist realism

BBC, 18, 21, 172–4
Ben, Philippe, French journalist, 65, 95
Beria, L., 15, 20
Berman, Jakub, member of the Polit-bureau, his influence, 15, 20, 22, 30, 38–9; his 'resignation', 41; his self-criticism, 125; attacks on him, 126
Bierut, Boleslaw, First Secretary of the PZPR, background and career, 14–15; and the secret police, 20–2; speech at III Plenum, 25; architect of Stalinism, 30; his death and funeral, 32–4; protected Gomulka and Berman, 125
Bor-Komorowski, General, 5–6
Breslau, *see* Wroclaw
Bruk, Michal, 35
Bulganin, Marshal, 61, 62
Bulgaria, 33
Bydgoszcz, 114

Catholic Church, *see especially* 149–158; Communist war on, 11, 69, 81; first indication of changed Com-munist policy towards it, 141; supports Gomulka during elections, 184–5; Party criticism of recon-ciliation with, 190
Catholics, 11, 140, 156–7, 182, 184
Censorship, 29, 31, 41, 56, 77, 137–8, 170–1, 175, 177
Chalasinski, Professor, expert witness at Poznan trial, 73–4
Charles X, King of Sweden, 67
China, 69, 167, 183
Chou en-Lai, 183
Church, *see* Catholic Church
Churchill, Sir Winston, 6–7
Collectivization (*see also* Agriculture), 12, 43, 100–1, 105–6, 151, 189
Communist Party of Poland (*see also* PZPR), 8–9, 32
Compulsory deliveries, *see* Agriculture
CPSU (*see also* Soviet Union), XX Congress, 32–4, 83, 102; on the Poznan riots, 53; leaders' visit to Warsaw, 88, 90; talks with the Poles, 90–7; communiqué on the talks, 91; reports on the talks to the VIII Plenum, 92–3; strained rela-tions with it, 119; demands for disclosure of reasons for visit, 135
Cracow radio, 143, 171
Cultural policy, 27–8
Curzon Line, 7
Cyrankiewicz, Jozef, Premier, back-ground and career, 15–16; on Bierut, 33; on democratization, 40, 54, 70–1; on the Poznan riots, 54, 71–2; on economic policy, 60–1; leads the progressives, 64; prepares Gomulka's return to Power, 82–3; in talks with the Soviet leaders, 90, 96; on the mood of the workers, 117–18; on Polish-Soviet relations, 118–19, 144; gains popularity, 133; receives delegations, 133; on the Natolin plot, 143–4; announces Government changes, 161; confers with officers, 161; answers Klosie-wicz's question, 166; elected to the *Sejm*, 186; his increased stature, 195
Czechoslovakia, 159–161
Czestochowa, 67–8